JunkGypsy

PURVEYORS OF THE — WORLD'S FINEST JUNK

ESTABLISHED 1998

Designing a Life at the Crossroads of Wonder & Wander

AMIE SIKES AND JOLIE SIKES

TOUCHSTONE

NEW YORK LONDON TORONTO SYDNEY NEW DELHI

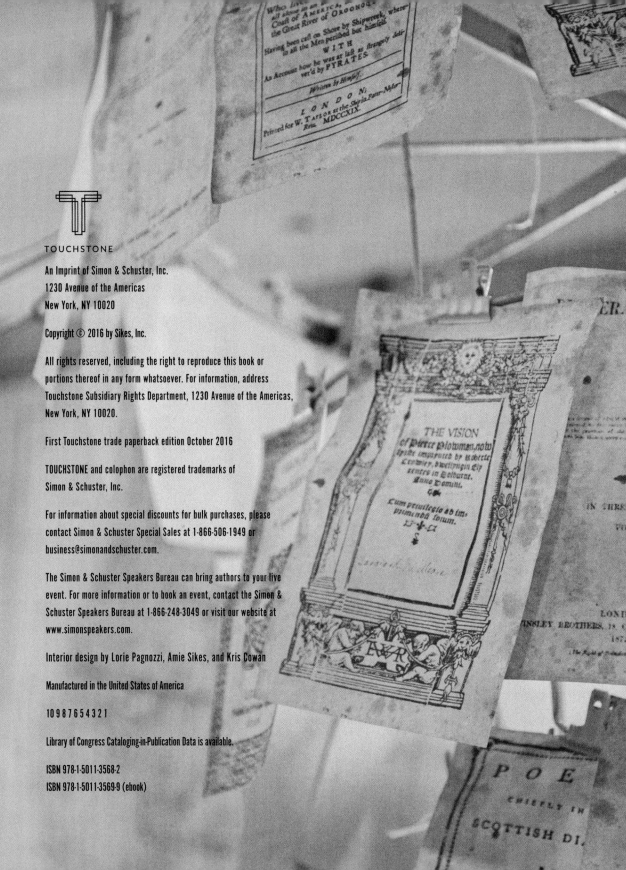

TOUCHSTONE

An Imprint of Simon & Schuster, Inc.
1230 Avenue of the Americas
New York, NY 10020

First Touchstone trade paperback edition October 2016

TOUCHSTONE and colophon are registered trademarks of
Simon & Schuster, Inc.

For information about special discounts for bulk purchases, please
contact Simon & Schuster Special Sales at 1-866-506-1949 or
business@simonandschuster.com.

The Simon & Schuster Speakers Bureau can bring authors to your live
event. For more information or to book an event, contact the Simon &
Schuster Speakers Bureau at 1-866-248-3049 or visit our website at
www.simonspeakers.com.

Interior design by Lorie Pagnozzi, Amie Sikes, and Kris Cowan

Manufactured in the United States of America

10 9 8 7 6 5 4 3 2 1

Library of Congress Cataloging-in-Publication Data is available.

ISBN 978-1-5011-3568-2
ISBN 978-1-5011-3569-9 (ebook)

TO OUR FAMILY—MOM, DAD, TODD, CASH BAKER, AND INDIE

CONTENTS

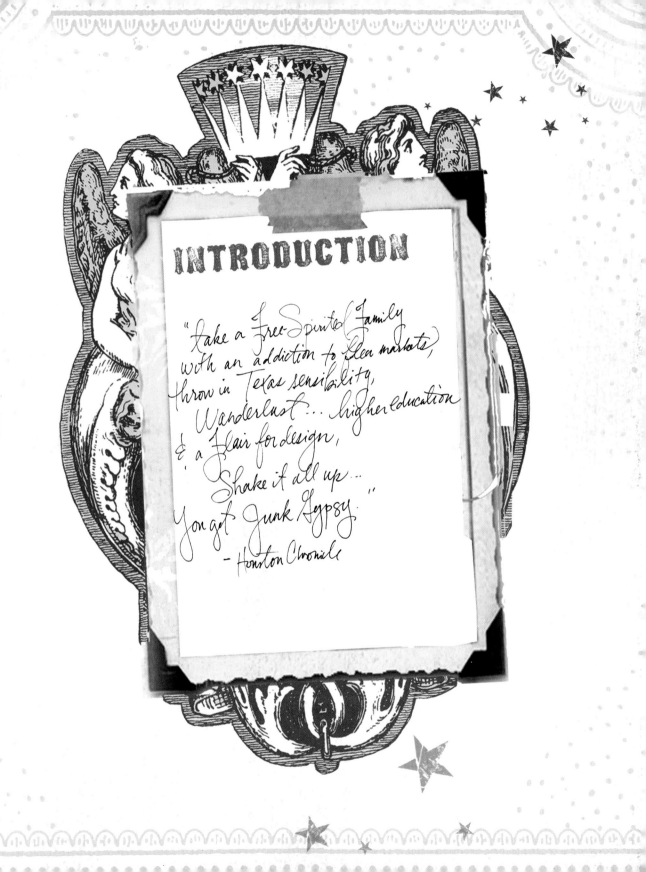

INTRODUCTION

"Take a Free-Spirited Family
with an addiction to flea markets,
throw in Texas sensibility,
Wanderlust... higher education
& a flair for design,
Shake it all up...
You get Junk Gypsy."

— Houston Chronicle

WELCOME TO GYPSYVILLE!

WE ARE THE JUNK GYPSY COMPANY, purveyors of the world's finest junk. Junk Gypsy is our family. Our business. Our love. Our inspiration. Our salvation. Junk Gypsy is the wild-hearted rogue who led us astray. It's what we created. It's what created us.

Our first book has been seventeen-plus years in the making, and we're so excited to have you along for the ride. You are family now. We've stayed up late nights that turned into early mornings. We've shed tears of joy and frustration. We've meditated, cogitated, and Kumbaya'ed. It's been nothing short of blood, sweat, and tears. (Seriously, we may need therapy.) Above all, it's been heart and soul. It is us. It is you. It is family and junk and big dreams and—lest we forget— Willie Nelson. Oh yeah, and tacos. Extra spicy.

This book is inspired by the three elements most important to Junk Gypsy. **The road: where we get our inspiration. The flea market: where practical magic meets elbow grease. Home: where our hearts are.**

We hope that by the time you get to the last page of this literary road trip, you'll be inspired to create, build, work, and play in a world that is totally true to you and your journey. We'll introduce you to the tools and techniques, show you hundreds of examples to spark your creative spirit, and offer step-by-step instructions on DIY projects for all you brave do-it-yourselfers, from creative beginners to hard-core craftsfolk.

To the dedicated, true-blue, boot-stompin' JG warriors who've been around since the beginning: Pull up a chair and stay awhile. We could never thank you enough. We've worked hard to keep this book as authentic to our JG spirit as you would expect it to be. We want you to love it: Highlight, dog-ear, and doodle in the margins. Take notes and tuck them in your mirror frame.

This book is for you.

To those who are picking up this book, wondering, *What's a Junk Gypsy and why is there a vintage chandelier in the back of their pink Chevy Suburban?*: Don't worry, we'll have you slinging glitter, wielding power tools, and navigating the flea market in no time. Welcome to our wild, wonderful neck of the woods! This book is for you!

To all of you starry-eyed dreamers who know the agony and ecstasy, the humility and beauty, the fight and exhaustion, the sacrifice and reward of entrepreneurial rainbow-chasing and windmill-tilting:

This book is for you.

Our story is worth its salt. It's about the gospel of the road, lessons learned under burned-out lights at beat-up tables in the corners of smoky bars. It's legend and lore of the most magical place on earth—the flea market—but most of all, it's about doing what beckons to your soul.

It is about adventure and life and friendship and love. Our story. Your story. So dream on.

—AMIE AND JOLIE
ROUND TOP, TEXAS
AUTUMN 2016

OUR STORY.
YOUR STORY.
SO DREAM ON.

WITH MOM IN THE JG TENT AT TEXAS ANTIQUES WEEK.
WE DIDN'T REALLY HAVE A PURPOSE FOR THESE MARCHING
BAND HATS FROM THE FLEA MARKET, BUT WE COULDN'T
RESIST THOSE RED PLUMES.

THROW OFF THE BOWLINES. SAIL AWAY FROM THE SAFE HARBOR. CATCH THE TRADE WINDS IN YOUR SAILS. EXPLORE. DREAM. DISCOVER.

—UNKNOWN

We believe there exists a restless roaming spirit deep within all of us. It's in our nature, in our very being: a yearning for that feeling of freedom, of letting go, of endless possibilities and of being the captain of your own destiny, the seeker of your own Holy Grail, a pirate on an endless quest for the golden treasure. Because the greatest parts of the road trip are the spontaneous, unplanned pit stops—the greasy-spoon roadside diners, the endless historical markers, and the waiting-to-be-discovered side roads. It's a mysterious, romantic thing to set out on a journey with no destination. No GPS. No phones. No computers. No meetings or conference calls. Just the road and its infinite wonder.

Long ago, we learned to listen to our gypsy souls, because when we do, inspiration comes on strong. It blows through our hair as we drive down the road, hums in our ears, glides through our fingers. It races ahead of us and follows behind us. It's the journey we fell in love with. The journey stole our hearts long ago and never let go. For us, the road—the wild blue yonder—beckons in our dreams, begs us from the passenger seat, and navigates our voyage. The mystery of taking a new trail—the discovery of a hidden junk store, the chance meeting of the waitress at the diner—lets you know you're on the right path. A path that found you. A path that, if you let it, becomes part of your story forever.

"IF A GIRL WANTS
SHE SHOULD JUST GO

"TO BE A LEGEND,
AHEAD AND BE ONE."

—CALAMITY JANE

AMIE

My sister, Jolie, and I never got comfortable with the "supposed to" part of life. You know, the part where you're "supposed to" go to college, you're "supposed to" settle down, you're "supposed to" get *real jobs*, and you're "supposed to" install granite countertops and crown molding. And luckily, because of our parents, we were never expected to. We grew up building forts in the woods (with lime-green shag carpet dragged out of the dump, thank you very much), digging old bottles out of the creek, riding horses, and playing Indiana Jones. I sewed dresses for my dolls out of scraps, but I also caught lizards, raised tadpoles, and shot cans with a pellet gun. My "anything boys can do, girls can do better" sister, Jolie, landed at the ER for stitches more than once pretty much every summer. We both bear battle scars as proud badges of honor that prove our dirt-under-our-fingernails childhood. Ground zero for our future.

I went to college and loved it. Got my journalism degree. Stomped through three years of straitlaced office life at the Texas State Capitol and was accepted to law school—a source of major concern for Mom, who's probably the only parent on the planet who'd weep at the idea of her elder daughter becoming an attorney. She felt it was a misuse of my creative spirit, and I knew deep down she was right. And while Texas politics is unbelievably exciting, it just wasn't the right fit for me. I was a country girl out of water. A "messy-haired" dreamer in a flat-ironed sea of networking.

So I turned down law school, plotted my escape, quit my job, and moved home. My dreams were big. My drive was unstoppable. I didn't know what I wanted to do, but I knew I wanted to do it my way.

JOLIE

Following your heart doesn't necessarily come with a PhD behind your name, and I discovered that this doesn't compute in the world of academia. I had earned an undergraduate degree and worked in Houston for several years, and then—despite an undeniable feeling of restlessness—got my master's in health and nutrition, desperately hoping it would cure my road-sick blues; hoping it would tame my inner wild child.

Then Dad got diagnosed with leukemia, and in that moment, my world crashed in on itself. I was working as an academic advisor at Texas A&M, and when I asked my boss if I could take off two days a month to help out at the family restaurant, the response was a flat no.

So against all common sense to some, I did then what I do now. I did what Mom and Dad taught us to do. I followed my heart. I quit my job, knowing it was the last time I would ever ask permission to be with my family.

Looking back, it seems odd that my husband, Todd, never questioned my decisions that often had unpredictable outcomes. Undetermined destinies. His faith equaled my own, and mine equaled Amie's, and together, we were all ready to conquer the world.

So now I was moving on . . . to become a junker. To officially become partners in crime with my mom and sister.

FROG-HUNTING CIRCA 1983 AT THE FAMILY FARM IN ARKANSAS. (*NO FROGS WERE HARMED IN THE MAKING OF THIS BOOK!*)

THE BEST BET MOM EVER MADE

When my sister, Amie, first left Austin, she started conjuring ideas, working part-time at the family pizza place, making wreaths out of grapevines, and designing crazy pillows. She scoured this newfangled thing called the Internet for business ideas. Her journals were filled with entrepreneurial stories and ideas, sketches and news clippings. There was a steady flow of inspiration despite the fact there was no steady paycheck.

Mom was the most unlikely accomplice. She was relentless, never stopping for a minute to say, "Wait, I paid for college and my daughter is building birdhouses in the backyard?" It takes a person who is oblivious to keeping up with the Joneses—a person who grew up with nothing yet built a beautiful life—to have the confidence to believe in something that hasn't happened. Something that might never happen. She was the no-nonsense person who knew all it takes is a little bit of faith and a whole lot of hard work. She knew this firsthand, from her hard-knock days being raised by a single mother with three jobs and living in the government projects in Commerce, Texas, to the day she and our dad decided to live life on their own terms and opened their own restaurant. She made pizzas all day and was at school at every afternoon to pick us up, driving to football games at night with sauce still on her shirt.

TOP LEFT ★ JOLIE SLINGING PIZZA WITH DAD AFTER SHE LEFT HER JOB. FROM ACADEMIC ADVISOR TO RED APRON IN ONE FELL SWOOP. *TOP RIGHT* ★ A VINTAGE RADIO FLYER WAS THE PERFECT VEHICLE FOR MOM AND AMIE'S MAIDEN VOYAGE TO THE FLEA MARKET WITH A PILE OF RAG-FRINGE PILLOWS. *BOTTOM* ★ OUR FIRST OFFICIAL JUNK GYPSY PHOTO SHOOT TOOK PLACE AT THE RESTAURANT IN OVERTON, WITH TODD BEHIND THE POINT-AND-SHOOT CAMERA AND DAD HOLDING A CLAMP LIGHT, CIRCA 2000.

TOP LEFT ★ DAD AND AMIE SETTING UP OUR FIRST BIG TENT AT TEXAS ANTIQUES WEEK IN 2000. *TOP RIGHT* ★ GREAT JUNK SCORE IN GROESBECK, TEXAS. GIANT FIBERGLASS TULIPS OFF AN OLD PARADE FLOAT. *BOTTOM* ★ STACKIN' 'EM HIGH AND DEEP IN *SANFORD AND SON* TRADITION.

But lucky for us, Mom loves the penny slot machines. She raised golden retrievers and saved the money as her "special gambling stash" for the occasional trip to Vegas. This is where fate steps in.

Mom told Amie, "I have two thousand dollars. Let's go to the flea market, sell your pillows, and buy some junk to refinish and sell. We could make a little money while you figure out what you want to do."

This turned out to be the best bet Mom ever made.

About five years after Amie left Austin, I followed in her tire tracks and left Houston. We agreed that we'd never seen a city looking so beautiful as it did in our rearview mirrors. We never could get used to the sight of skyscrapers on the horizon instead of towering pines. We missed the stars. Our cowgirl boots longed for the earth. Some indefinable *something else* was calling to our gypsy souls.

THE MORAL OF THE STORY

My sister and I are dreamers and rebel yellers, artists and happenstance inventors, cowgirls and never-say-die workaholics. At the end of the day, we have our individual differences and our common weaknesses, but therein lies our strength. Where one leaves off, the other begins. Amie and I truly do "complete each other"—in a non-Hallmark kind of way. We never stop to have a sister moment about it, because we're always hell-bent and hurtling toward a common goal. We're driven by an unearthly force that pushes us to make Junk Gypsy everything we ever dreamed it could be.

OUR DESIGN PHILOSOPHY

EXACTLY WHAT DO JUNK GYPSIES DO?

We get that question a lot.

Short answer: There's not much we haven't done.

Long answer . . . well, that's a bit more complicated. A many-splendored thing, you could say. We built a business in the fields of the flea market, searching for secondhand junk, which we restore, repurpose, and resell. We also design tees and jewelry emblazoned with quotes and images that inspire us. We have a 7,000-square-foot store—the Junk Gypsy World Headquarters in Round Top, Texas—but our customers around the globe can shop with us 24-7 at Gypsyville.com. Our most recent addition is the Wander Inn on the back forty of our property.

We tend to find ourselves embroiled in crazy design projects that involve Airstream trailers, tour buses, weddings, and events for celebrities and other extraordinary people. A few of our greatest hits: Airstreams for Billie Joe Armstrong of Green Day, Dierks Bentley, and Miranda Lambert; a wedding reception for Miranda Lambert; a Hotel California–themed artist lounge for the Austin City Limits Music Festival headlined by the Eagles; a line of JG-designed cowgirl boots; a host of awesome girl decor for Pottery Barn Teen; our very own Junk Gypsy paint; and a Sweet 16 party for Sadie Robertson—not to mention multiple charitable events at which we've been able to donate significantly to causes near and dear to our hearts.

All our projects have one thing in common: We bring kindred spirits together. We work from our hearts. We work from our souls and from our roots. We try to make something spectacular out of something that seems, at first glance, not so spectacular. We are junkers to the core, and we have inadvertently become designers. We love what we do. And we do what we love.

SO WHAT IS JUNK GYPSY STYLE?

We love the unexpected, the gloriously chaotic combination of a million different elements. We love things that have history. We're not looking for perfection. If we love something, we will find a way to make it fit.

We love rock 'n' roll style as well as farmhouse. We love boho and hippie and country. The truth is, we're a little of all those things combined. You could say we have commitment issues. We love color, but we also love white. We love vintage concert posters mixed with red-lacquered Asian pieces, then combined with chippy, peely farmhouse furniture and maybe topped off with fringed velvet curtains.

For us, the design process is a gut-wrenchingly beautiful thing, a deeply meditative process, a cultural exploration of who you are, and it's one of the most personal things you can do. If a home is set up the right way, there's something you can feel, and it's not for anyone else; it's for yourself. All the stars (or the chandeliers) align, and you just know: *It's right*.

Every time Jolie and I design for someone else, we do a sort of individual immersion into that person's life. We want to know his or her past, dreams, passions, and alter egos. We want his or her home to be an escape. A little piece of salvation. We want it to be fun. Sentimental. Personal.

Our dad coined the term "funky shway" to describe this total alignment of yourself with your surroundings. A place where you put your favorite concert ticket stub framed on the wall along with a vintage piece of art. And then feel the freedom to paint your walls turquoise blue.

We believe in very few hard-and-fast design principles. We have one rule: There are no rules.

WITH **WILLIE NELSON** AS YOUR NAVIGATOR
JACK KEROUAC AS YOUR NORTH STAR
AND **THELMA** AND **LOUISE** RIDING SHOTGUN
YOU KNOW THIS TRIP IS **BOUND FOR GLORY**

OUR GUIDING LIGHTS

Sir Isaac Newton said, "If I have seen further, it is by standing on the shoulders of giants." We're reminded daily of the many pioneers, trailblazers, wordsmiths, and brave groundbreakers who've walked this walk before us: the poets, songwriters, creators, and inventors. The rule-breakers and the daydreamers who dared to be different and to color outside of the lines. The ones who took the road less traveled and made all the difference. (Thank you, Robert Frost.) When we study the lives and paths of those before us, we're infinitely inspired. We learn. We endeavor. We dream. Here's to you; here's to them. May we all be trailblazers in ways great and small.

 A FEW OF THE TRAILBLAZERS WHO'VE TRAVELED THE PATH BEFORE US, LIGHTING OUR WAY AND PROVIDING AN ENDLESS SOURCE OF INSPIRATION:

★ ALBERT EINSTEIN

★ WILLIE NELSON

★ HONDO CROUCH

★ WALLY BYAM

★ RACHEL ASHWELL

★ TRACY PORTER

★ RICHARD BRANSON

★ BERYL MARKHAM

★ AMELIA EARHART

★ THELMA & LOUISE

★ SONORA & HER HIGH-DIVING HORSE

★ JACK KEROUAC

★ ST. CHRISTOPHER

★ DOLLY PARTON

★ ANNIE OAKLEY

★ THE SUFFRAGETTES

JUNKER'S TOOLBOX

First things first. Here are a few essentials we think everybody should have around—many of which will come in handy as you tackle the DIY projects in this book.

DIY *Hammer Legend*

PRO TIPS

Our quick and dirty tips we've picked up from a lifetime of building, salvaging, and re-creating:

- Use candle wax on drawer edges and runners inside the chest. They'll glide right open.

- Dawn dish soap will dissolve grease on almost anything.

- Invest in a good orbital sander. You can thank us later, when you see how much easier life is.

- Sunshine and a little bleach water are the best fix for odiferous drawers.

- Bar Keepers Friend is the best way to polish any metal object that needs some shine.

- Love your mistakes. We're like the Julia Child of DIY. We make plenty of mistakes, but we keep moving forward. Sometimes they turn out to be accidental genius.

- Sign and date your DIY projects in a hidden place. It's like a hidden gift for the person who will inherit that object down the line.

- Mix and match hardware if you don't have a complete set—or even if you do.

- Dry brush hardware in different colors to bring out the ornate details or update old pieces.

- This ain't a tattoo; it's paint, glitter, and glue. Be fearless! Have fun!

- Galvanized pipes fitted with appropriate elbows and flanges make perfect curtain rods, towel bars, and toilet paper holders. Ask a friendly pro to thread the ends for you at the hardware store.

- Wood glue and clamps are your friends for tightening up wobbly joints. Use a syringe to inject glue into hard-to-get places under veneer and into other tight spots.

- Always carry leather gloves in your vehicle. You never know when you might have to pull an old rusty chair out of the Dumpster on your way to the movies. (Yes, this has happened.) Oh, and get a tetanus shot every few years.

- It's a scientific fact: Dirt is good for your immune system and your frame of mind. And DIYs make for great family time, which is good for your soul.

- The Golden Rule of DIY can't be said often enough: Measure twice, cut once.

LOOK FOR THE ⊤ WITH EACH PROJECT

⊤ = EASY

⊤⊤⊤ = TOUGH

⊤⊤ = CHALLENGING

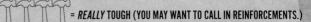

⊤⊤⊤⊤ = *REALLY* TOUGH (YOU MAY WANT TO CALL IN REINFORCEMENTS.)

DASHBOARD THERAPY

Get out there and get back to the asphalt. Get a little highway Zen. Go west, young woman, take in all the great sights of the open road, and get a great big dose of dashboard therapy.

Let us never forget how important it is to get out of our element every once in a while—to get on the road, to take a different route—and no road trip, great or small, is complete without epic road tunes. It doesn't matter if you're on a transcontinental adventure or heading across town to visit the folks. Roll the windows down, crank the music up, and let those lyrics run through your head and through your veins. We go for the original troubadours: the shakers, the changers, from rock 'n' roll to old-school honky-tonk. Music breathes fresh energy into our creative spirit. Being in this place—this is where great ideas are born.

THIS SHOULD GET YOU

ROGER MILLER ★ "KING OF THE ROAD"

JERRY REED ★ "EAST BOUND AND DOWN"

JOHN DENVER ★ "TAKE ME HOME, COUNTRY ROADS"

ROBERT EARL KEEN ★ "THE ROAD GOES ON FOREVER"

JANIS JOPLIN ★ "ME AND BOBBY MCGEE"

WILLIE NELSON ★ "ON THE ROAD AGAIN"

WAYLON JENNINGS ★ "LUCKENBACH, TEXAS"

STEVIE RAY VAUGHAN ★ "TEXAS FLOOD"

JIMI HENDRIX ★ "LITTLE WING"

MIRANDA LAMBERT ★ "AIRSTREAM SONG"

MERLE HAGGARD ★ "MAMA TRIED"

ELTON JOHN ★ "TINY DANCER"

FROM HERE TO THERE

THE ALLMAN BROTHERS BAND ★ "SOULSHINE"

BOB DYLAN ★ "LIKE A ROLLING STONE"

VAN MORRISON ★ "INTO THE MYSTIC"

THE DOOBIE BROTHERS ★ "BLACK WATER"

THE BAND ★ "THE WEIGHT"

STEPPENWOLF ★ "MAGIC CARPET RIDE"

DWIGHT YOAKAM ★ "LITTLE SISTER"

GUY CLARK ★ "L.A. FREEWAY"

B. B. KING ★ "LUCILLE"

JERRY JEFF WALKER ★ "MR. BOJANGLES"

MUDDY WATERS ★ "HOOCHIE COOCHIE MAN"

ZZ TOP ★ "I'M BAD, I'M NATIONWIDE"

DIY 🔨 Ombré Cactus

You can't go wrong with psychedelic spray paint, a piece of scrap wood, and a cactus stencil. Consider this neon therapy. Spray those worries away, honey child, and then stand back and realize that if Jimi Hendrix had hired a decorator, it mighta been you!

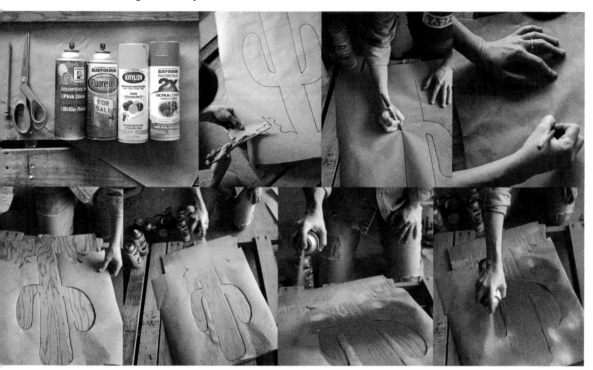

1 Trace design on kraft paper or poster board. We used a regular pencil for this, but you may want to outline in Sharpie if you can't see it well enough for cutting.

2 Cut out design with scissors.

3 Use double-stick tape to secure stencil to wood or canvas.

4 With broad strokes, spray horizontally, switching colors as you move up the stencil.

PRO TIP: WE LIKE TO KEEP COLOR FAMILIES TOGETHER. FOR EXAMPLE: GREENS AND BLUES FADE INTO PURPLES AND PINKS, THEN REDS, ORANGES, AND YELLOWS.

TRAVEL-INSPIRED DIYS

All roads lead home. Gear up with a good pair of gloves and some tin snips and let your imagination roam free.

CLOCKWISE FROM TOP LEFT ★ A RETRO CAR LIGHT COUPLED WITH A ZEN GLASS TERRARIUM. ★ A CHROME HEADLIGHT RIM FROM A '57 CHEVY MAKES AN UNCONVENTIONAL MIRROR FRAME. ★ OLD LICENSE PLATES ACCENT WALL ART, A CEILING FIXTURE, AND AN OUTSIDE-THE-BOX SEATING AND STORAGE BENCH. ★ TO MAKE THIS UNIQUE LAMPSHADE, SET A GLOBE IN A FIVE-GALLON BUCKET AND CUT AROUND THE RIM WITH A JIGSAW.

LARGE MARGE: TRANSFORMATION AND TRANSPORTATION

Large Marge spent her early years at Overton Independent School District. We took many a school road trip in that white Suburban. It was used for FFA events, UIL meets, tennis and track teams, and other random school trips. When the day came for her to be replaced with a shinier, newer ride, Marge (she didn't know it then, but that was her name) was put up for auction. Luckily, Mom and Dad were at that auction. They bid $300 and walked away proud owners of a 1980 Chevy Suburban, complete with torn seats, a dry-rotted dashboard, and, of course, no power locks or windows.

Mom and Dad rescued ol' Marge and gave her a new home with our family. Dad thought she might be useful at our family farm in Arkansas, but when they brought her home, we loved her and knew that she was meant for adventure, a superhero of junky epic proportions. She wasn't meant for the scrapyard, but for great celestial things.

We decided she must be pink. With horns on the front. And flames down the sides, and pink-striped curtains, lots of bumper stickers, and—obviously—a chandelier.

BROKE DOWN ON A COUNTRY ROAD. EVERY ONCE IN A WHILE, MARGE INSISTS ON STOPPING TO SMELL THE ROSES.

WE ADDED CHANDELIER CRYSTALS
TO A SILVER PLATTER AND THEN
MOUNTED A NEW INTERIOR DOME
LIGHT.

RIGHT ★ MIRANDA'S VINTAGE GUITAR
WAS SIGNED BY MERLE HAGGARD, WHOSE
MUSIC INSPIRED THE WHOLE DESIGN;
VINTAGE PIANO SHAWL CURTAINS FROM
THE FLEA MARKET; JG CUSTOM BEDDING.
LEFT AND ABOVE ★ VINTAGE CRAZY QUILT
BEDSPREADS; ANTIQUE TAPESTRIES MADE
INTO PILLOWS; CRUSHED VELVET CURTAINS.
THE LOVE LETTERS ABOVE THE SINK ARE
AN HOMAGE TO MIRANDA'S SONG "LOVE
LETTERS." *BOTTOM* ★ FAUX ALLIGATOR
CHAIRS AND CEILING ADD ROCK-STAR VIBES
TO THIS COWGIRL'S TOURING HAVEN ON
WHEELS.

MIRANDA LAMBERT'S TOUR BUS

The only people who log more miles than junkers are long-haul truckers and country music singers. The road is an integral part of the country music tradition.

In 2003, a hell-raising country girl and fellow East Texan appeared on the country singing competition show *Nashville Star*. Miranda Lambert's unique sound was filled with passion and twang. We anxiously watched and cheered her on every week—and not only because she was our landslide favorite. Her accent sounded like home. There's something about an East Texas drawl; you can spot it anywhere. And us East Texans, we stick together.

We didn't know it then, but our paths were destined to cross. After the competition, Miranda's star was rising, and—through a series of fortunate events—we realized we had sort of a mutual admiration society going. Before we knew it, we were on the phone with Bev, Miranda's mom, discussing ways we might collaborate. Soon after, the guns-and-wings logo was born, followed by a multitude of other designs, followed by the tour bus, and the list goes on and on. . . .

And we've become soul sisters.

We go together like fried bologna sandwiches and nacho-cheese Doritos. Like Pancho and Lefty. Big Red and beef jerky. Our families share a history and are forever connected as friends. Junk Gypsy is permanently emblazoned on her arm as the creators of her guns-and-wings logo and tattoo. We have laughed and cried together. Danced and worked together.

We've also road-tripped halfway across the country in Miranda's tour bus, which we decked out for her in true Junk Gypsy style.

"THERE AIN'T NO RULES HERE. WE'RE TRYING TO ACCOMPLISH SOMETHING."

—THOMAS EDISON

JUNKOLOGY

CHAPTER 2

We knew about junk as a way of life way before we knew about it as a way to make a living. Mom was and remains to this day a relentless, never-say-die fan of all things old. Hands down, the reason we love junk—the reason Junk Gypsy exists—is because of Mom. She always believed old stuff had more character, more soul. She sees beauty in the most unlikely places.

To Mom, the value in an object isn't determined by the price tag; it's determined by your love for it. From gumball-machine trinkets to vintage TV trays, Mom's passion for thrift goes back to her childhood, when resale shops, garage sales, and thrift stores were a way of life out of necessity. She instilled the love of old in us when we were just kids. We couldn't help but see a world of possibilities all around us.

Basically, Mom was junky when junky wasn't cool.

We always ask people, "How'd you get into the junk business?" Everyone has a different story, but there's always a common thread: transformation. Falling into the cosmos of the flea market and never turning back.

One story that's always stayed with us: "I went to Canton Trade Days one weekend back in the seventies. I had a carload of old treasures and some random odds and ends from a hippie

TOP LEFT ★ WHO DOESN'T NEED A TWELVE-FOOT-TALL NEON COWBOY RIDING AN ARMADILLO? *TOP RIGHT* ★ THE RUSTIEST ITEM AUTOMATICALLY CATCHES JOLIE'S EYE. THE BEST PART OF BEING A JUNKER IS THE THRILL OF THE HUNT. *BOTTOM* ★ A BEAUTIFUL DAY AT TEXAS ANTIQUES WEEK IN ROUND TOP. TENTS LINE THE HORIZON AT TIN STAR FIELD.

road trip between Saint Louis and Texas, and I just needed some cash. So I pulled up at the flea market in my old truck with my flatbed trailer full of quilts. I love the energy on quilts. Someone made each and every piece with their hands, with fabrics that meant something to their family. There's an energy there. I set up my space and went to sleep that night on my flatbed trailer underneath an old quilt, looking up at the Texas stars. Next morning, I awoke before sunrise, and I had an out-of-body experience. I could still barely see the stars in the morning sky, and I could see all the tents and the flea market that still lay sleeping, and I knew for the first time in my wandering life that I had come home. And I've never left."

It's that moment. The moment when you've come home. It's the moment we all live for. You're like a musician transformed by the magic of music, who drank the proverbial Kool-Aid, looked into the eyes of destiny, and with a wild heart full of possibilities, you stay the course. Regardless of the fame, fortune, or peril—never mind the life it may or may not offer. It's a drunken, glorious elixir that captures your soul, whether you're a shopper or a vendor. You feel the trueness of the flea market resonate beyond all reason, and you too have *come home*.

That's what happened to us, and that's why starting Junk Gypsy wasn't really an option: It was our destiny. It was the only thing for us. Once the flea market found us, we were going to do anything and everything to figure out a way to stay in that magical, marvel-filled world. And we always will.

SECONDHAND INSIGHTS

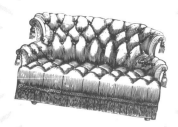

SAFETY FIRST ★ SANITY SECOND ★
AND A FEW OTHER THINGS IT'S GOOD TO KNOW WHEN
YOU INVITE JUNK INTO YOUR LIFE. APPLY AS NEEDED
TO LIFE AND FLEA MARKETING.

THERE'S A DIFFERENCE BETWEEN SHOCKING AND ELECTRIFYING: Using old chandeliers can be tricky—and dangerous. Be sure to have a certified electrician check or replace old wiring.

GETTING OLD IS NOT FOR SISSIES: Old stuff is usually built solid. Cosmetic issues and minor breakage might make it look like it belongs on the curb, but don't pass something up because of a few simple fixes. It might have good bones, and that's what counts.

IN RUST WE TRUST: We love rusty things. Just add a coat of water-based polyurethane to preserve that beautiful natural aging process.

IT'S WHAT'S INSIDE THAT COUNTS: Used couches and chairs are often cloaked in ripped, torn, or stained fabric at the flea market. If the chair or sofa has a good shape and good lines, envision it upholstered in a different fabric.

THE END JUSTIFIES THE MEANS: Sit in every potential chair or couch. Looks can be deceiving and a little rehab goes a long way. The one that looks comfy might make your life miserable, and the one that looks like heck might be comfortable enough to justify a makeover.

IT'S THE INVISIBLE GIFTS THAT KEEP ON GIVING: The scent of cat pee, rat pee, cigarette smoke, or roach droppings will sometimes never, ever come out. Don't kid yourself. Sunshine and bleach spray will do a lot, but often the strongest of smells will prevail. And no piece of furniture in your home needs to be wafting that around.

Distressing Furniture

DIY ⚒ *Basic Distressing*

There's nothing like the natural look of "oldness" on a piece of vintage furniture. We love every square inch of old paint, every glorious shade of rust, every dent or crack that makes that piece unique. Of course, not all old furniture comes with that perfect shade of chippy-peely grandeur; some must be lovingly liberated from their humdrum life. Three essential tricks of the trade: basic distressing, white glue (crackle) technique, and dry brushing.

1 Prep your surface by sanding lightly. This will remove existing paint or polyurethane and give your paint a rough surface to adhere to.

2 Apply a base-coat of paint, and allow it to dry.

3 Apply two coats of a second color, and allow that to dry for at least twenty-four hours, depending on climate.

4 Sand strategic areas. Hit the areas of natural wear and tear to create a distressed effect.

White Glue Technique

DIY 🔨 White Glue (Crackle) Technique

1 Prep the surface, wiping it down to remove dust, barn grunge, or other residue.

2 Paint with base coat color and allow to dry.

3 Brush white school glue over the base coat. A thicker coat of glue results in larger cracks. Apply a thin coat if you want fine cracks.

4 Brush on the top coat of paint while glue is still wet.

5 Allow your project to dry completely.

Dry Brushing

DIY ⊤ Dry Brushing

1 Wipe down the surface to get rid of dust and dirt.

2 Using very little paint on the brush, lightly sweep the surface. Imperfection is your goal. You don't want a smooth, uniform surface, so keep that brush dry!

PRO TIP: IF THE OBJECT YOU'RE PAINTING HAS NOOKS AND CRANNIES, DON'T DIG IN THERE WITH YOUR BRUSH. GO EASY, AND LET THE IRREGULAR SURFACE DO SOME OF THE WORK FOR YOU.

PAINTING PRO TIPS

IN THE RIGHT HANDS, PAINT HAS THE POWER TO TRANSFORM A DATED YARD-SALE FIND OR RESCUE A SOLID PIECE OF FURNITURE FROM THE CURB

SURPRISE YOURSELF: Buy mis-tints at your hardware or home improvement store to save big money. Sometimes the "oops" shelf has a color you don't know you want until you see it. Come up with your own custom colors by mixing leftover paints instead of throwing them out. What have you got to lose? If you don't like it, you can easily paint over it or try another blend.

MIX IT UP: Add white to any color to soften the tone or lighten the shade. Add water to white paint to make your own whitewash. Add sand for texture or fine glitter to make your own sparkle finish.

FINISH FINE: Our favorite finish for furniture is a flat finish like our chalk and clay paint. It distresses great, but you'll need to use a sealer. If you want to skip the sealer step, use a satin finish. Occasionally, the moment calls for a high-gloss finish like a fire-engine-red lacquer. Just remember, high gloss is harder to sand if you want to distress.

GO NATURAL: Use clay- and chalk-based paint or milk paint. Olive oil or coconut oil works as a sealer or furniture polish. Make your own natural stains with tea and coffee. Soak steel wool in vinegar for a rust-infused tint. And at the end of the day, mix coconut oil with sugar to create the perfect natural scrub for those DIYer hands.

COLORFUL EXPRESSIONS
A FEW OF OUR FAVORITE GO-TO PAINT COLORS

★ BEHR "CANYON CLOUD"

★ RALPH LAUREN METALLIC "OYSTER"

★ SHERWIN-WILLIAMS "GYPSY RED"

★ RALPH LAUREN METALLIC "HIGHGATE"

★ JUNK GYPSY PAINT "WANDERLUST"

★ JUNK GYPSY PAINT "GYPSY PROM"

★ SHERWIN-WILLIAMS "REAL RED"

★ JUNK GYPSY PAINT "BUTTERMILK BISCUIT"

★ BEHR "MINT MAJESTY"

★ BEHR "SWEET RHAPSODY"

★ BENJAMIN MOORE "SIMPLY WHITE"

SIGNS, SIGNS, EVERYWHERE SIGNS

Our love for vintage signs goes back to our childhood in the restaurant business. Mom and Dad were scooping up vintage signs and neon back when nobody wanted them. Here are a few of our favorite signs, some keepers, and some that got away.

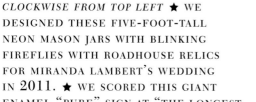

CLOCKWISE FROM TOP LEFT ★ WE DESIGNED THESE FIVE-FOOT-TALL NEON MASON JARS WITH BLINKING FIREFLIES WITH ROADHOUSE RELICS FOR MIRANDA LAMBERT'S WEDDING IN 2011. ★ WE SCORED THIS GIANT ENAMEL "PURE" SIGN AT "THE LONGEST YARD SALE" IN THE SMOKY MOUNTAINS. ★ THIS RETRO-STYLE DRIVE-IN SIGN IS NEW BUT A GREAT WAY TO ADD VINTAGE FLARE. ★ THIS 1950s DOUBLE-SIDED LIGHT-UP STAR STILL SHINES. THE CLASSICS NEVER GO OUT OF STYLE. ★ THERE'S SOME DEBATE OVER WHETHER THESE SIX-FOOT SPECS CAME FROM AN OPHTHALMOLOGIST'S OFFICE OR AN ADULT VIDEO STORE. EITHER WAY, IT'S ONE OF OUR FAVORITES! ★ TODD SANDERS OF ROADHOUSE RELICS DESIGNED THIS CROWN FROM FOUND OBJECTS FOR THE JUNK-O-RAMA PROM, AND IT NOW STANDS PROUDLY IN OUR STORE.

"IF YOU BUILD IT . . ."

IF YOU BUILD IT

CHAPTER 3

We set out to find a great business, and we found a great life. We made it up as we went along, Dr Pepper cans and business magazines strewn on our floorboards. Opportunities presented themselves like hitchhikers, standing by the road with their thumbs out.

We've danced the soles off our boots by the light of the Round Top moon, played extras in a *Friday Night Lights* episode, and felt the spirit of Johnny Cash at the Country Music Hall of Fame. Our souls were deepened at an East Texas home-goin' where the hallelujahs and amens were like a hearty helping of soul food. We've changed tires on the side of half the back roads in Texas, stood speechless on sacred ground at Sun Studio, and felt the ghost of Elvis at Graceland. We got lost in Compton, discovered arrowheads in the hills of Arkansas, hiked with hippies in the foothills of California, and were mesmerized by the magic of a Smoky Mountain sunrise. We ate fried chicken at the House of Blues in Chicago and fried pickles at the rustiest, crustiest roadside diners this side of the Mississippi. We walked the red carpet in our cowboy boots, got to see Reba McEntire sing karaoke, and accidentally ended up at a Kanye West party. We've loaded trailers in the rain, in tornadoes, and in sleet. We've hauled junk in the mud, snow, and muck.

We felt like we could conquer the world.

Our online sales were growing by leaps and bounds. Our design projects were expanding, powered purely by word of mouth, and our customer base was more than just customers: They were a passionate, loyal tribe of women and men, young and old. A rabid underground following

CLOCKWISE FROM TOP LEFT ★ CHILLING IN OUR AUSTIN CITY LIMITS ARTIST LOUNGE. ★ STRUTTING THE RED CARPET WITH MOM AND DAD AT A MACY'S EVENT AT THE ORPHEUM IN CHICAGO, 2007. ★ GREETING LONGTIME JUNK GYPSY SHOPPERS ANGIE AND KELLY.

formed before our very eyes. They would be at every show, every flea market, every event to which the road led us. They became like family. We knew them by name, knew their kids' names and which college their kids were heading off to. We provided dorm decor, birthday goods, and wedding ideas. We would celebrate small victories together, always cheering one another on in our individual quests for the pursuit of junk and living life on our own terms. In short, it was the organic creation of an authentic brand. Nothing was planned and nothing was forced. We were doing what we loved. And we got a lot of love back.

After five years of setting up at flea markets, we had a long discussion about "what normal people would probably do next." We decided to open a store in Tyler, Texas. We found the perfect location, painted the walls, and had display pieces ready. But at the last minute, we walked away. The road wasn't through with us yet. It was calling, and we had to go. We still had adventures to conquer, people to see, junk to collect, lessons to learn. In the words of Louis L'Amour, one of our patron saints: "The trail is the thing, not the end of the trail. Travel too fast and you miss all you are traveling for." The road is more to us than just a stretch of black asphalt. More than just a means to an end. More than just a mile marker on the way to a predetermined destination. It's a crystal ball that holds all the answers.

In 2002, we decided it was time to put down virtual roots. We faced some surprisingly fierce opposition. Back then, the tech world didn't take too kindly to out-of-the-box creative ideas of what a website should look like. Specific cookie-cutter models existed, and anything outside that template was considered utter doom in the digital world. Clearly, we aren't template kinda girls, so we did what we had to do. We fought for what we wanted. We hunkered down and applied noses to cyber-grindstone, learning what we needed to in order to make our online home as much a reflection of ourselves as the homes where we hang our actual hats. We cared more about the experience and less about the in-your-face-selling stuff.

Over the next ten years, as we created Junk Gypsy, Junk Gypsy was creating us. Challenging us. Daring us. The road was paved with hard work and persistence, and the way hasn't always been smooth. But we've gotten good at sticking to our guns. We come from a long line of rule breakers, men and women who believed in the power of their individual voices and opinions. You have to fight for that which you love. And we have fought for Junk Gypsy every step of the way.

CLOCKWISE FROM TOP LEFT ★ SPORTING PETTICOATS AND COWGIRL BOOTS FROM OUR FIRST-EVER PHOTO SHOOT. ★ EVEN THE LITTLEST GYPSIES FIND SOMETHING TO LOVE AT THE FLEA MARKET. ★ HANGING OUT WITH LONGTIME JUNK GYPSY SHOPPER AND FRIEND SHEILA AT THE JG TENT. ★ SCREENSHOT FROM OUR FLEDGLING RENEGADE WEBSITE. ★ WE DIDN'T GET FAR ON THIS BICYCLE BUILT FOR TWO, BUT BIKES ARE ALWAYS A HOT COMMODITY AT TEXAS ANTIQUES WEEK, SO IT DIDN'T LAST LONG IN OUR TENT.

the Junk Gypsy

WELCOME TO GYPSYVILLE!
THE RAUCOUS AND ROWDY HOME OF GYPSIES,
JUNKERS, DREAMERS AND TRUE-BLUE REBELS!

THE JUNK GYPSY COMPANY, WITH THEIR TROUPE OF TALENTED
SCAVENGERS, TRAVELS NEAR AND FAR TO FIND ROADSIDE TREASURES,
DECADENT DECOR AND EXOTIC GOODS FOR YOUR HOME.

AND OUR TEAM OF REBELLIOUS DESIGNERS WORK TO BRING YOU
SPUNKY COUTURE THROUGH THE JUNK GYPSY TEES,
JEWELRY AND OTHER CHARMING WEARABLES.

SO WITH A LITTLE WANDERLUST IN YOUR SOUL AND
A ROGUISH GLEAM IN YOUR EYE JOURNEY THROUGH
OUR WILD AND SPIRITED WORLD!

ENJOY THE RIDE!

JUNK GYPSY
PURVEYORS OF THE
WORLD'S FINEST JUNK

JUNKGYPSY WORLD head quarters

6365 SIXTH STREET • COLLEGE STATION • TEXAS • 77845 • 979-776-5951
WWW.GYPSYVILLE.COM

SANCTUARY

Ideas, dreams, and sketches for the Junk Gypsy store gradually took shape. As junk conservationists, we considered it our duty to create a preserve for wild junk, a habitat in which every species of junk could coexist harmoniously and symbiotically. In 2012, we broke ground in Round Top, Texas, poured concrete, and started building the Junk Gypsy World HQ we had dreamed of for so long.

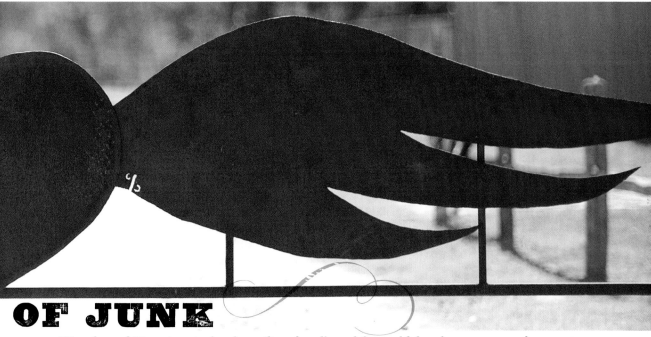

OF JUNK

We salvaged Victorian tin for the ceiling, beadboard from old farmhouses across the county, a six-foot-wide Spanish chandelier for the entrance, and crazy huge corbels. We bought a pair of chippy, peely pink-and-white doors salvaged by way of Dead People's Stuff from an old man named Hootie in Asheville, North Carolina. When you enter the hallowed halls at the House of Blues, you see a placard that says, "Take with you a piece of our soul, leave with us a piece of your heart." We hope the same for anyone who walks through our doors.

TOP LEFT ★ AMIE'S INITIAL VISION FOR OUR STORE. *TOP RIGHT* ★ AN EPIC DAY IN JG HISTORY. CASH BAKER AND INDIE LEAVE THEIR HANDPRINTS TO FOREVER MARK THE MOMENT IN 2011. *CENTER* ★ OUR LOCAL COWBOY FRIEND CRAIG BAUER HANDCRAFTED OUR HEART-WITH-WINGS IRON GATE FOR THE ENTRY INTO GYPSYVILLE. *BOTTOM LEFT* ★ GRAND OPENING AT GYPSY WORLD HQ IN SPRING 2014. *BOTTOM RIGHT* ★ BARE TREES AND A BUILDING WITH GOOD BONES GET READY TO BLOSSOM IN SPRING.

JUNK KARMA

Junk karma is real. Junk karma is good vibes and good Zen and the passing of junk from one person to another. It's the righteous rescue of something that was bound for the burn pile, the spiritual renovation of that piece, and then the passing of that piece to another person's home. Reborn and repurposed. The salvation of one person's trash into another's treasure.

CLOCKWISE FROM TOP LEFT ★ HERE WE MIX THE ROMANTIC COWGIRL LOOK WITH A CLAY POT FROM MEXICO AND A BEJEWELED LONGHORN. ★ IN EVERY SECTION OF THE JG STORE, WE LIKE TO TELL A STORY BRINGING OLD AND NEW TOGETHER. OUR *OUT OF AFRICA*–INSPIRED VIGNETTE SHOWCASES A VINTAGE ITALIAN BED UNDER A SAFARI TENT WITH A CRYSTAL CHANDELIER. ★ WE MADE CACTUS MARQUEE LIGHTS OUT OF PLYWOOD FOR OUR BORDERTOWN SECTION FEATURING A GENUINE WEST TEXAS TUMBLEWEED, AN OLD CAR FRONT WITH WORKING HEADLIGHTS, AND A PERFECTLY RUSTED WINDMILL. ★ THE VAULTED CEILING IN THE STORE IS MADE ENTIRELY FROM SALVAGED CORRUGATED TIN, THE PERFECT BACKDROP FOR A GRAND SIX-FOOT IRON CHANDELIER.

ARCHITECTURAL SALVAGE 101

Whether it's as small as a doorknob or as big as the whole door, architectural salvage brings a sense of history and old-world craftsmanship into your home. It can be eco-friendly, thrifty, and just plain cool, and it's not nearly as intimidating as it sounds, if you know a few tricks of the trade.

A BIG OL' STORE COUNTER FROM THE 1800S MAKES AN ORNATE AND FUNCTIONAL ISLAND FOR A FARMHOUSE KITCHEN.

SEAL THE DEAL: Most architectural salvage has lead-based paint. We like to seal salvage pieces with a water-based clear coat to reduce any flecking or peeling.

BATTLE OF MISFITS: Measuring is critical if you're trying to fit an old piece into an existing structure. Old doors and windows are great, but they're typically smaller than new ones, so be sure you know your dimensions.

DON'T FORGET THE LEFTOVERS: Columns, corbels, and capitals make great focal points in a room and can be used a variety of ways.

HEAVY METAL: Salvage hardware is a great addition to cabinets, doors, and drawers.

REINVENT THE WHEEL: If you love a salvage item but it just doesn't fit your space, get creative and use it in a whole new way. Old corbels make great shelving or bookends. Windows function as picture frames, doors as tabletops, an old gate as a headboard. Step back and let that found treasure speak to you.

MAKE IT WORK: Raw materials vary. You've got to sit down and think it through, channeling your inner tactical engineer. Ask for advice. Ask for help. Recognize that "one size fits all" is a myth. When you're working with old stuff, every project is unique. You'll have to reinvent the wheel a little, but that's part of the fun.

INDIAN ARCHES, TRACTOR-SEAT STOOLS, AND MISMATCHED BARN BOARDS
WORK AND PLAY TOGETHER IN A BEAUTIFULLY HIP KITCHEN.

PROJECT *Salvage Tree House*

This is one of our favorite projects with architectural salvage. Our good friends Amy and Brian Kleinwachter, from Old World Antieks, built an amazing tree house that we were lucky enough to help decorate. From our gold wings on the front of the tree house to the funky design ideas inside, this little dwelling in the branches is built almost entirely from salvaged items and serves up a Texas-size helping of DIY inspiration!

CLOCKWISE FROM TOP LEFT ★ A CEDAR STUMP WITH AN OLD PHONOGRAPH HORN CREATES A UNIQUE NATURAL AMPLIFIER WHEN YOU DOCK YOUR IPHONE IN THE SLOT. ★ THE FRINGED BUTTERFLY CHAIR IS FROM OUR POTTERY BARN TEEN LINE. ★ IMPORTED CRATES SERVE AS FUNKY SHELVING. ★ AN UNEXPECTED MIX OF SOFT, HARD, AND HOMEMADE BRINGS IT ALL TOGETHER.

THE WANDER INN

The Wander Inn is our lodge on the back forty of the Gypsyville compound, which is located close to the original Chisholm Trail. It's a place to dream big and dream loud while surrounded by Texas longhorns. Combining the spirit of the great western cattle drives with incurable wanderlust, the Wander Inn is about all the things we love: the road, the flea market, the music, the country. For the gypsy in all of you: welcome home.

CLOCKWISE FROM TOP LEFT ★ CLASSIC JG JUXTAPOSITION (DAD CALLS IT "FUNKY SHWAY"): A MODERN BAR SINK IN A VINTAGE STORE COUNTER WITH AN ORNATE MIRROR AND GALVANIZED BARN LIGHTS. ★ SALVAGED RETRO MOTEL SIGN, 1960s GLITTER VINYL CHAIRS, AND A STENCILED ROADIE BOX. ★ LONGHORNS PRETTY MUCH GO WITH EVERYTHING. ★ *CLOCKWISE FROM LEFT ON FOLLOWING PAGES* ★ AN OLD HEADBOARD FROM MEXICO PAINTED WITH JG "DREAMCATCHER" AND SANDED FOR A DISTRESSED EFFECT. ★ VAULTED CEILINGS HOST ROUGH-HEWN BEAMS AND AN OVERSIZED CHANDELIER. ★ GILDED CHAIRS AND A GLITTER FEATHER LAMPSHADE. ★ HEADBOARDS FROM SALVAGED WOOD, STENCILED AND PAINTED OMBRÉ STYLE.

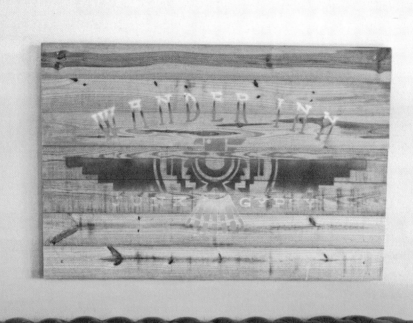

DIY 🔨🔨 *Ombré Wall*

Waking up to the colors of a West Texas sky or a sun-bleached Ventura casita—that's how this ombré wall feels to us. It starts out electric and ends up serene. The gradient technique captures that worn-out-West-Texas-sky look and evokes a feeling of lazy days on the veranda, sunsets off the Great Barrier Reef, and hazy Gulf Coast afternoons.

1 Pick four colors of paint, ranging from dark to light, within the same color family.

2 Trim wall with painter's tape, and use a roller to paint entire wall with the lightest hue.

3 Paint a bottom panel eighteen to twenty-four inches tall with the darkest color.

4 Paint the panel right above that with your second darkest color.

5 Blend the lines between these two panels with a dry brush technique, alternating between the two colors. Your goal here is to create a seamless gradient between the two colors. This works better with two people, so grab a friend to help!

6 Duplicate this process, working your way up until the entire wall is painted, blending the colors together as you go. Your finished ombré effect will be amazing!

BEHIND THE SCENES

Almost fifteen years into the evolution of Junk Gypsy, we took a wild ride into the world of TV. It was never part of our plan, but it became an important detour. For three seasons now, we've junked, roadside stopped, and DIYed our hearts out on HGTV and Great American Country. And we learned some pretty darn valuable life lessons along the way.

It's best to test-drive a new idea (e.g., Dierks Bentley's resin table) before you try to pull it off in front of millions of people.

Never eat fried pickles on camera.

When all else fails, go for the glitter.

CLOCKWISE FROM TOP ★ ON STAGE IN FRONT OF SIXTY-FIVE THOUSAND PEOPLE AT THE CMA MUSIC FESTIVAL. WE WERE GETTING USED TO THE CAMERAS, BUT THIS TOOK NERVOUS TO A WHOLE NEW LEVEL. ★ ON SET WITH HGTV FILMING THE "ENDLESS YARDSALE" SPECIAL IN TENNESSEE. ★ JOLIE SOUNDS THE SIREN ON OUR FIRE TRUCK TO KICK OFF JUNK-A-PALOOZA. ★ IT'S GO TIME! FILMING THE GRAND OPENING AT JG WORLD HQ IN ROUND TOP IN 2014. ★ JOLIE IS FOREVER THE QUEEN OF SOCIAL MEDIA. HERE SHE MAY BE SNAPCHATTING, INSTAGRAMMING, PINTERESTING, TWEETING, PERISCOPING, VINING, OR ALL OF THE ABOVE.

"THE DIFFERENCE BETWEEN AN ADVENTURE AND AN ORDEAL IS ATTITUDE."

—ROBERT LIPKIN

Pat, Diane, Phillip, Janie

CLOCKWISE FROM TOP LEFT ★ MOM AND DAD WITH MOM'S BROTHER, PAT, AND SISTER, DIANE, ON THE RIVER IN ARKANSAS, CIRCA 1952. ★ MOM AND DAD WITH THE KIDS AT THE FAMILY FARM IN ARKANSAS ★ IN THEIR COURTIN' DAYS. THAT BRIEF, SHINING MOMENT BEFORE WE CAUSED HIM TO LOSE HIS HAIR.

CHAPTER 4

This is the story of the Gypsy and the Cowboy. . . .

The youngest of seven boys, our dad, Phillip Sikes, was born and raised in southern Arkansas, *waaaaaay* out in the country where the pine trees are tall, the twang is thick, and the Little River dances through the farm. There was no indoor plumbing, no air-conditioning, and no video games, just wide-open spaces and ponds and creeks and cows and everything else a little boy needs to let his imagination run free.

Janie Patterson grew up like a Texas gypsy, moving from town to town. She and her older sister and brother were raised by a hardworkin' single mom who always held multiple jobs at one time. Mom had a wild spirit and a beautiful way of bending the rules. Growing up, Mom spent her summers in Arkansas, where her favorite playmate was a cowboy about her age. His name was Phillip.

They spent many summer days together, baling hay, cane-pole fishing, riding horses, having fried-chicken picnics, and cruising in Mom's brother's convertible. The gypsy and the cowboy got married, had two daughters, and moved to Memphis. Life was sweet and good.

We were living in Memphis, Tennessee, in 1977, the year Elvis died. Dad was working as a sales rep for a big chemical company. Mom was selling BeautiControl at night, driving around the not-so-swanky parts of Memphis giving home parties. Dad's boss came to town, and Mom and Dad had him over for dinner. They were expecting the boss to announce that Dad was getting a big promotion, so Mom bought fancy glasses that cost five dollars each.

She still has those five-dollar glasses.

As it turns out, the boss was not there to give Dad a big promotion. He was there to tell them that the branch was closing and Dad was out of a job.

Grit doesn't happen when things are good. Grit happens when we're tested. When Elvis is dead, and things are bleak at best, because you're out of work, you have two toddlers, and you just spent a precious twenty bucks on something not vitally necessary.

Mom and Dad sat down that night and had a real come-to-Jesus about what they wanted their lives to be. They went back to Texas and began their careers as lifelong entrepreneurs. Their endeavors—including the pizza restaurant where we cut our teeth—were always successful on one level or another; we never had new cars or a swimming pool in the backyard, but come what may, they knew they could always depend on each other, and they would always captain their own destiny.

Grit.

It's part of who we are. Who we are meant to be. How we were raised.

One of the most important things we were taught was *how to work*. When you do something yourself, with your own two hands, the intrinsic value increases exponentially. It is one of the core principles in the JG Mantra of DIY: Your pride in the end result is directly proportional to the amount of work and dedication you put into the project.

We were taught the value of down-and-dirty, sweat-on-your-brow, muscles-achin', back-breakin', baby-needs-a-new-pair-of-shoes physical labor. It's a little thing called "sweat equity." Elbow grease. Good old-fashioned "get in there and get it done." And thank goodness, because now we're more intimidated by long lines at the shopping mall than we are by our JG job requirements.

After Amie and I both fled our big-city jobs, we immersed ourselves in the back-to-basics world of building and creating. We both kept journals bursting at the seams with our individual business ideas, with our thoughts and inspirations. Amie ventured into pillow making and furniture rehab, while I created a line of eco-friendly scented rocks, among other things, a business I called Sister Moon. This was great therapy for both of us: the sacred process of using our hands to create something. Our hands and our heads needed to be busy. We needed to create. To work. When we get in a rut, there's nothing more exciting than ditching the technological duties and pulling on the work gloves. It's an essential component to our business and our mental health.

There's something about being out of your office, away from your desk, disconnected from the Internet, and reconnecting with the rewards of manual labor. Working with your hands, your head, and your muscles. There's something noble about accomplishing something concrete. Something you can feel and see and pat yourself on the back for.

When you put in a little sweat equity, it makes the work all the sweeter.

DIY 🔨🔨 Log Table

This is one of our favorite nature-inspired DIYs.

1 Acquire appropriate-size stumps. We shoot for twelve-inch to eighteen-inch diameter stumps for side tables. Remember: Bigger isn't necessarily better here—unless you have a tractor or forklift to move a giant stump. (This is a great time to commission help from someone who's handy with a chain saw!)

2 If you have the time, it's best to store the wood in your garage or barn for about a month to let it dry. This also helps loosen the bark.

3 Get to stripping! The bark, that is. Not you. It's best not to DIY naked. Not that we know from experience. The difficulty of this step is determined by the type of wood you are working with. Cedar pulls off nice and clean. Oak requires a *lot* more elbow grease. You can use a variety of different tools for this step: hammer, pry bar, paint scraper, chisel, or bark spud. Whatever safely and effectively works for you.

4 Be a smooth operator! Use a sanding block or just pieces of sandpaper to smooth out the stump. *Really* smooth.

5 Wipe down your stump to get all the sawdust off.

6 Finish it off with three to four coats of water-based polyurethane. Tip: You can also use wood stain if you want to give your stump some color other than its natural wood grain.

7 Top that sucker off with a Shiner Bock!

DAD'S BUTTERMILK BISCUITS

A moment of silence, please . . . Here in the South, certain things are held sacred: giving thanks, Friday-night football games, and homemade buttermilk biscuits cooked in the oldest cast-iron skillet you can imagine. Dad's been perfecting his bread recipes for as long as we can remember, and let me tell ya, they're worth getting up for.

Dad's mama was famous in all of southern Arkansas for her yeast-rise cinnamon rolls, and Dad spent many an hour helping her knead, pat, and roll her dough. To him, bread is a science and an art. A deliciously beautiful art! Man may not be able to live by bread alone, but I can't get enough of it. Give me bread or give me death. Especially Dad's bread—sourdough, yeast-rise, homemade pizza dough, cinnamon rolls, buttermilk biscuits, and holy-moly-the-best-crispy-southern-style-cast-iron-skillet cornbread you've ever had in your life.

2 cups flour	½ tsp baking soda	5 tbsp real unsalted butter
4 tsp baking powder (Dad prefers non-aluminum powder like Rumford)	½ tsp salt	1 cup + 2 tbsp buttermilk

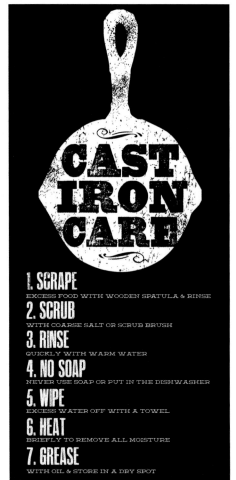

CAST IRON CARE

1. SCRAPE
EXCESS FOOD WITH WOODEN SPATULA & RINSE

2. SCRUB
WITH COARSE SALT OR SCRUB BRUSH

3. RINSE
QUICKLY WITH WARM WATER

4. NO SOAP
NEVER USE SOAP OR PUT IN THE DISHWASHER

5. WIPE
EXCESS WATER OFF WITH A TOWEL

6. HEAT
BRIEFLY TO REMOVE ALL MOISTURE

7. GREASE
WITH OIL & STORE IN A DRY SPOT

1. Preheat the oven to 450°F.

2. Stir together dry ingredients in a bowl.

3. Cut 4 tbsp of the butter into dry ingredients.

4. Add buttermilk.

5. Stir to form moist dough.

6. Flour hands and knead lightly.

7. Melt the remaining 1 tbsp of butter in iron skillet in oven.

8. Pinch off biscuits (little larger than a golf ball), place in skillet.

9. Bake 18 minutes or until golden brown.

10. Enjoy southern comfort food at its best!

PRO TIP: DAD LIKES TO ROLL THE FORMED BISCUITS IN THE MELTED BUTTER BEFORE PLACING THEM IN THE SKILLET.

DIY 🔨 *Teepee*

This is one of our favorite outdoor projects with the kids! It's simple, gets back to the basics, and creates the coolest play space ever.

1 Pick the perfect spot in your yard, woods, or neighborhood greenbelt.

2 Gather ten to fifteen tall branches to serve as the main frame of the teepee.

3 Prop the branches together to form the frame. Tie some of these together with jute or twine to reinforce your structure.

4 Using loppers, trim branches from any trees or shrubs that you want to incorporate into your teepee.

5 Place the branches into the frame, starting at the bottom and working your way up. They should lay over one another like fish scales. Attach them to the frame with jute as needed.

6 Finish it off with a grapevine door frame and indoor-outdoor twinkly lights to create a super-magical effect when the sun goes down.

ABOVE ★ LOADING OUT OUR TENT AT TEXAS ANTIQUES WEEK AFTER A TORRENTIAL DOWNPOUR WITH HELP FROM ARCHIE AND LINDSEY. *LEFT* ★ SPELLING OUT OUR FAVORITE WORD IN THE ENGLISH LANGUAGE. HEY, Y'ALL, IT'S LOAD-OUT DAY!

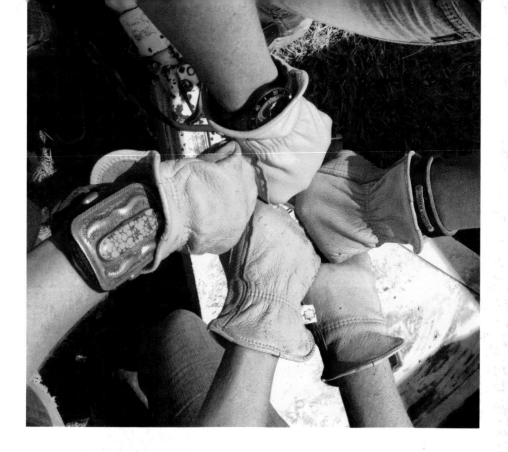

GIRLS AT WORK

Our dad's mom was a trailblazer. She left home for nursing school, cut her waist-length hair off at her chin in an act of rebellion, and went on to become a country nurse, farm wife, mom of seven boys, and—lest we forget—bread baker extraordinaire. When the dinner bell rang at their house, there was always enough for the boys at the table and the stranger at the door, because in the country, that's just the way you do things. Mom's mom, Granny Helon worked in the war factories, as did thousands of American women, helping keep the military well supplied. These women were dubbed Rosie the Riveters, an early icon of women's economic independence.

We feel as though everyone is buoyed up by a good honest day's work and we've seen firsthand that girls can do anything they set their minds to. We've loaded trailers in the rain, sleet, muck, and mud with a mostly all-girl crew at times, and their never-say-die attitude is the thing that makes all the difference.

PROJECT *Shot-to-Hell Can Lights*

Jolie isn't a girly girl, although she was homecoming queen. Don't tell her I told you. She likes to forget about anything that involves standing up and being recognized in front of people. She, like me, is more of a back-row person, even though JG has kinda taken us outta that place.

In high school Jolie ran around town in our dad's hand-me-down, beat-up truck, lovingly named Sanford. (And that was way before we knew we were gonna grow up and basically be Sanford and Son—only with a lot more sequins and fringe.) Anyway, Sanford had a seat that wouldn't stay locked, so it just rattled back and forth, which made pulling up to the stoplight and trying to act cool basically impossible. Instead of some boring new ride, she preferred the truck with a story. A dirty, beat-up story.

Jolie can cook a mean—and I do mean *mean*—loaf of homemade bread and just about anything else you'd like. But she also never wants to be called a decorator, and won't be caught dead wearing pink.

One of our all-time favorite DIYs came about quite accidentally: Jolie loves to target shoot. She can kill a can dead in about two seconds flat with a rifle. Other designers might carry around books of color swatches while taking on the task of designing one of country music's weddings of the decade. Not Jolie. She took to the fields with ol' Duke, her 20-gauge pump-action shotgun, and—channeling Miranda Lambert's "Gunpowder & Lead"—let the air outta some big monster cans. And that, folks, is how it's done.

Behold, the shot-to-hell can chandelier!

MARCUS LUTTRELL'S OFFICE

In 2005, Marcus Luttrell was brought home as the lone survivor of Operation Redwing. He was broken and battered but not defeated. His indomitable spirit and fierce loyalty has kept alive the memory and heroic service of so many soldiers. (Marcus told their story in his book *Lone Survivor: The Eyewitness Account of Operation Redwing and the Lost Heroes of SEAL Team 10*.) We're honored to know Marcus and are forever changed by his story of survival, his never-quit spirit, and his love for his state and his country. Our task was to create an office space in which he could find peace and inspiration. Where he could pen his thoughts in his many journals. Where he could sign books that find their way across the globe, inspiring others with his story of hope, valor, and authentic grit.

True grit.

We are inspired. Every damn day.

THIS DESK FEATURES "CHALLENGE COINS" GIVEN TO MARCUS AS A SYMBOL OF RESPECT FROM PEOPLE ALL OVER THE WORLD.

PITSTOP

Marcus Luttrell

The Meaning of "Grit"

My entire life I've had to work hard to reach my goals. I've never been the fastest, the smartest, or the strongest, but what I do have is the ability to take pain and to push through it. Whether it's doing something stupid with my friends in high school that got us in trouble but ended up teaching us a valuable lesson, or all the hard work it took advancing in martial arts, or getting into the SEAL teams or the things I've experienced while in the teams. What got me through was grit. To me grit is enough stubbornness to lead you to a successful path. It's never quitting on what you believe in. It's having pure determination and finishing. I always knew I wanted to be a husband and a dad, and grit has brought me to be who I am today. I'm a man who loves my family, I'm a man who will always remember and honor my fallen brothers, and I will never quit on anything I believe in.

WE SALVAGED LEGS FROM A GRAND PIANO AND HELD ON TO THEM FOR YEARS, WAITING FOR JUST THE RIGHT PROJECT. WE KNEW THIS ONE WAS SOMETHING SPECIAL.

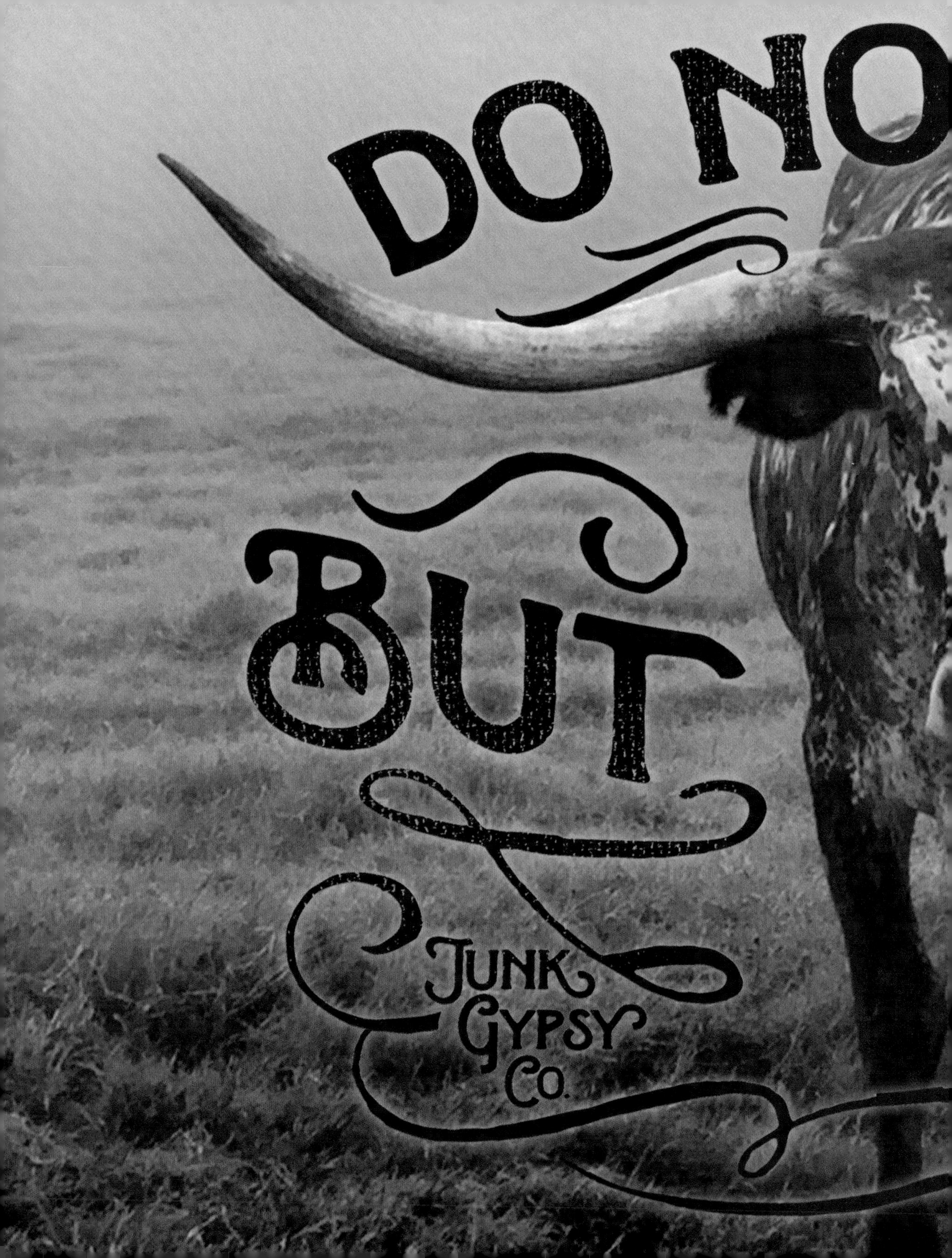
DO NO
BUT
JUNK
GYPSY
CO.

HARM

TAKE
NO
BULL

TEXAS

In *Travels with Charley*, John Steinbeck points out that "Texas is a state of mind." In fact, it goes way beyond that: For most Texans, it's akin to a religion. People either love the Lone Star State or hate it, but you won't find many who are on the fence. Texas inspires passion, one way or the other. There's a brash mystique about it, a vast, wild brand of beauty in an ornery climate that'll kill ya as soon as look at ya. In Steinbeck's words: "Rich, poor, Panhandle, Gulf, city, country, Texas is the obsession, the proper study, and the passionate possession of all Texans."

Not all who wander are lost

—J. R. R. TOLKIEN

MAGIC IN A TIN CAN

CHAPTER 5

Airstream: an American-designed, American-made American dream. Each one has its own story to tell. We love this American symbol of freedom. Airstream was founded in the wake of the Great Depression by Wally Byam. To us, the iconic Airstream became a symbol of a better way to get from here to there, literally and figuratively.

After more than eighty years on the road, Airstreams remain timeless. They embody the great American road trip. Peek inside that shiny tin can and you might find the Griswolds on a family vacation or rock stars in a jam session. Glistening like a shooting star on the highway of our life, the Airstream is more than an icon for us: It's become a huge part of what we do. We relate to that head-in-the-clouds, feet-on-the-ground vibe. They're dreamy yet practical.

Outfitting the ultimate Gypsy transport is all about those two things. These architecturally beautiful aluminum ships that sail the byways are so well built and sturdy, we've been able to push the limits in every way and retrofit each one to transport its owner to a different place on the map and a different state of mind.

Working with a mobile structure that has round walls, hardly a straight line in sight, and limited weight capabilities presents all sorts of challenges. Securely hanging art, chandeliers, and architectural elements that are hundreds of years old is a complex feat of engineering. But in a

HANGING OUT IN FRONT OF THE AIRSTREAM WE
RETROFITTED FOR BILLIE JOE ARMSTRONG.

weird way, all these wild limitations bring out the impossible in us, inspiring ideas that can be incorporated in all kinds of small spaces.

After traveling around in our old RV to flea markets for years, fate intervened. Our good friend Miranda Lambert wrote "The Airstream Song," which was partly inspired by us. It was instantly clear that Miranda must have an Airstream of her own for her upcoming tour, which we had aptly named "Roadside Bars & Pink Guitars." Without any real knowledge of what we were doing (never stopped us before), we searched out a 1953 Airstream Flying Cloud. We had two weeks to transform it into a cosmic cowgirl saloon on wheels and make it functional for Miranda's *very first headlining* cross-country tour—a huge moment in the career of any musician.

So began the first chapter in our Airstream chronicles . . .

TOP ★ US WITH MOM AND DAD AND MIRANDA LAMBERT IN FRONT OF THE FIRST AIRSTREAM WE DECORATED. *MIDDLE* ★ AMIE AND INDIE IN THE LIGHT OF A GLOWING NEON AIRSTREAM OUTSIDE SADIE ROBERTSON'S SWEET-SIXTEEN BIRTHDAY PARTY.

TOP ★ THIS BABY IS AT HOME ON THE RANGE BUT BOUND FOR A LIFE ON THE BEACH. *BOTTOM* ★ A FLOCK OF BLOW-MOLD FLAMINGOS SHOWS UP FOR MIRANDA'S ROADSIDE BARS & PINK GUITARS TOUR IN 2010.

MIRANDA LAMBERT'S AIRSTREAM

Miranda's trailer was an ode to all that is grand, rhinestoney, and metallic turquoise in the world. It was fringe, glitter vinyl, and Sputnik chandeliers. The cosmic cowgirl trailer—later dubbed Wanda the Wanderer by Miranda—had a very specific mission in its latest incarnation: It was to be a rolling saloon on wheels, hauled behind her tour bus to every venue she played in the United States that year—which is a whole lotta traveling for this 1953 Airstream that had been all but put out to pasture.

We combined Miranda's needs with her personality: a Victorian sofa from the 1800s retrofitted with 1950s pink glitter vinyl, drum tables topped with old wood out of Texas's own legendary Dixie Chicken saloon, and last but not least, her very own rhinestone cowboy. This trailer needed to look really good at night, so we armed ourselves with BeDazzlers and rhinestones, and after a few burned-off fingertips, declared our mission accomplished.

LEFT ★ CASH BAKER, FIVE AT THE TIME, HELPED DAD WITH SOME BUILT-INS. DAD TOLD HIM THAT CARPENTERS ALWAYS SIGN THEIR WORK, SO UNBEKNOWNST TO MIRANDA, CASH BAKER'S JOHN HANCOCK IS SCRIBBLED INSIDE THE EXTRA SEATING THAT COVERS THE WHEEL WELL. *CLOCKWISE FROM TOP LEFT* ★ LIKE THE SONG SAYS: "HOMEMADE CURTAINS, LIVE LIKE A GYPSY." ★ THIS STATELY VINTAGE SOFA GOT A MAKEOVER WITH FRINGE, STUDS, AND GLITTER VINYL. ★ SACRED SALVAGE INCLUDED DRUM TABLETOPS MADE WITH WOOD FROM THE LEGENDARY DIXIE CHICKEN SALOON.

BEV LAMBERT'S AIRSTREAM

Bev Lambert, Miranda's mom, was so in love with Miranda's Airstream, Miranda decided to surprise her with an Airstream of her own. Miranda had the tour bus pick Bev up in the middle of the night. She woke up in Round Top to find Miranda, us, and her very own Airstream. It turned out to be the perfect place for Bev to get out of the day-to-day craziness of running Miranda's Pink Pistol stores and the MuttNation Foundation. And the perfect place for the two of them to go glamping.

CLOCKWISE LEFT ★ A CAPTAIN'S BED IS PERFECT FOR SWEET DREAMS AND EXTRA STORAGE. ★ GLAMPING DETAILS COMPLETE THE LOOK. ★ CONFIRMED NON-SEAMSTRESSES MIRANDA AND JOLIE STARTED WITH THE BEST OF INTENTIONS TO BE HELPFUL WHILE AMIE MADE CURTAINS, BUT ENDED UP WITH THIS LOVELY. . . WHATEVER THIS IS. *CLOCKWISE RIGHT* ★ HERE WE ARE, WITH MIRANDA, WAITING TO SURPRISE BEV! ★ AUTHENTIC VINTAGE SOUVENIR SALT AND PEPPER SHAKERS FROM NASHVILLE. ★ JG T-SHIRT PILLOW.

MAGIC IN A TIN CAN

DIERKS BENTLEY'S AIRSTREAM

Dierks Bentley wanted an Airstream that brought together the two most important things in his life. He wanted it to be one part songwriter/troubadour lair and one part camping hideout for him, his wife, and their three children. We did our due diligence: listened to hours of Dierks's music and came up with an Americana troubadour hideout that gave him everything he wanted. This was one of the bigger Airstreams we've done: a thirty-one-foot Sovereign Land Yacht with a bathroom and kitchen—and it turned out to be even more meaningful than we even suspected. As we added finishing touches, Amie sketched out a quick thunderbird for the drop cloth curtain on the back.

CLOCKWISE FROM TOP LEFT ★ STRIKING OUR BEST POSE WITH DIERKS. ★ AN OUTHOUSE-INSPIRED DOOR LEADS TO THE ULTIMATE PORTA-POTTY. ★ IN THE SPIRIT OF JUNK KARMA, A SALVAGED CHURCH PEW CUT IN HALF SERVES AS PERFECT BOOTH SEATING. WE RESURRECTED THE PEDAL BOARD FROM A GRAND PIANO FOR A SOULFUL TABLE BASE. CAN I GET AN "AMEN"? ★ A VINTAGE MINNOW BUCKET LIGHT SETS OFF THE RALPH LAUREN HIGHGATE METALLIC INTERIOR. ★ COZY SLEEPING QUARTERS WITH SALVAGE WOOD, SANTA FE—STYLE BEDDING, AND CHANDELIERS.

MAGIC IN A TIN CAN

CLOCKWISE FROM TOP LEFT ★ THE AMERICANA TROUBADOUR GALLEY FEATURES VINTAGE BUNTING, FRINGE CURTAINS MADE OUT OF DROP CLOTHS, AN OLD WOODEN CRATE WITH CASTERS ADDED FOR VERSATILE COFFEE TABLE STORAGE, AND LAST, BUT NOT LEAST, A HAND-STENCILED FLOOR. ★ WE CREATED A TABLETOP MADE OUT OF VINTAGE CONCERT POSTERS AND BAR TOP RESIN. ★ OLD-SCHOOL 8-TRACKS STAND THE TEST OF TIME. ★ INSPIRED BY LUCINDA WILLIAMS'S "SHARP CUTTING WINGS," WE CREATED A SCONCE OUT OF AN OLD MOTORCYCLE GAS TANK.

109

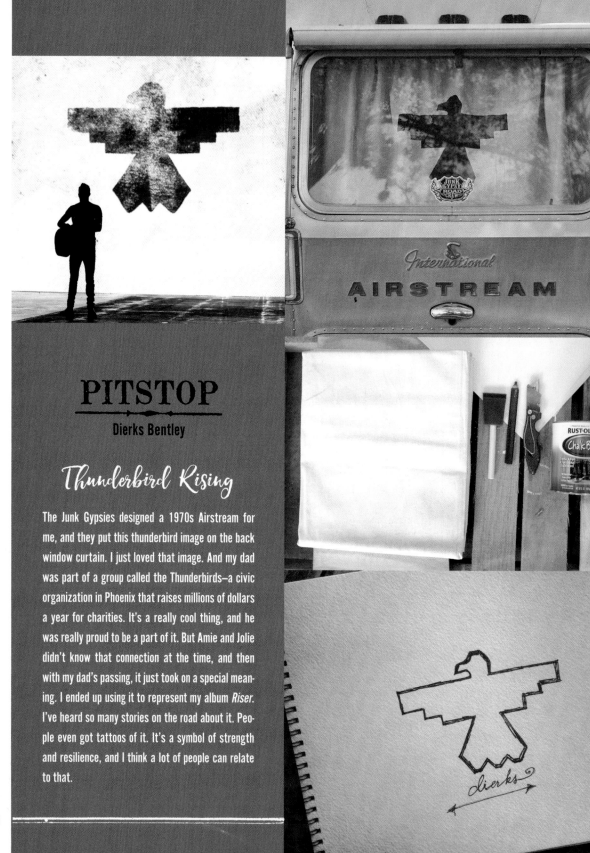

PITSTOP

Dierks Bentley

Thunderbird Rising

The Junk Gypsies designed a 1970s Airstream for me, and they put this thunderbird image on the back window curtain. I just loved that image. And my dad was part of a group called the Thunderbirds—a civic organization in Phoenix that raises millions of dollars a year for charities. It's a really cool thing, and he was really proud to be a part of it. But Amie and Jolie didn't know that connection at the time, and then with my dad's passing, it just took on a special meaning. I ended up using it to represent my album *Riser*. I've heard so many stories on the road about it. People even got tattoos of it. It's a symbol of strength and resilience, and I think a lot of people can relate to that.

DIY 🔨 *Thunderbird Curtain*

It's no secret we love drop cloths. They are essentially cheap giant canvases. Their uses are without limits. We created this stenciled curtain for Dierks Bentley's Airstream a few years ago. It's a perfect way to create your very own custom curtain.

1 Mark and measure the space where you plan to hang your curtain, and then cut the drop cloth about two inches larger than desired size. (Tip: Depending on how you plan to hang your curtain, you may need to leave more room up top.)

2 Wash and dry the drop cloth and lay it out on a flat surface.

3 Draw your image on poster board and cut it out with scissors or an X-Acto knife to create the stencil.

4 Place the stencil flat on the drop cloth. Be sure you leave enough room at the top for a curtain rod or other hanging device.

5 Using a sponge brush, dab paint inside the stencil. We like using chalkboard paint or flat paint for this project. Spray paint can be used as well; just be sure you apply at a ninety-degree angle to prevent seepage under the stencil. Less is more here, y'all. Too much paint on your brush causes the paint to bleed out under the stencil.

6 Let the drop cloth dry before you hang it. We know, you're eager to step back and envision yourself rolling down the road with Dierks Bentley and his band on their next tour, but be patient.

BONUS STEP FOR OVERACHIEVERS: If the image is reversible (words won't work unless they're the same coming and going, like "wow") flip the stencil, line up the image on the other side, paint, and let dry again. That way it looks equally awesome from inside and out!

CLOCKWISE FROM TOP LEFT ★ THE TRANSFORMATION BEGAN WITH VINTAGE RECLAIMED WOOD FLOORING. A FLEA MARKET CABINET HOUSES THE WHEEL WELL AND SERVES AS STORAGE. SNAKESKIN VINYL COVERS CABINET DOORS ABOVE THE COUCH. ★ WE MACGYVERED COUNTRY-GIRL SURFBOARD HOLDERS OUT OF HAND-TOOLED LEATHER STRAPS. ★ WE SPRAY-PAINTED A DEFUNCT SURFBOARD WITH A GUADALUPE STENCIL AND GAVE IT A REMOVABLE WOODEN BASE TO FUNCTION AS A PORTABLE COFFEE TABLE. ★ THIS WAS THE MOST STREAMLINED TRAILER WE'D EVER DONE. SALVAGED ARCHITECTURAL ELEMENTS INCLUDE A 150-YEAR-OLD INDIAN TEMPLE PIECE FOR THE BED NOOK.

BILLIE JOE ARMSTRONG'S AIRSTREAM

We start every Airstream project with a quote (or quotes): powerful words that act as a North Star as we navigate the choices and challenges. For Green Day's front man, Billie Joe Armstrong, we let Rumi speak to us: "Let yourself be silently drawn / by the stronger pull of what you really love."

These words—which Billie Joe has tattooed on his chest—could certainly apply to every Airstream and everything else we've ever done, but Billie Joe's trailer was a tad different for us, for a lot of reasons. It was a surprise, for one thing: a twentieth-wedding-anniversary present from Billie Joe's wife, Adrienne, affectionately called "80" by him and Green Day fans across the country. This trailer, like the others, had a specific mission: It was to be a Zen surf shack where Billie Joe could go to write and escape. So with four Green Day documentaries and a pile of CDs in hand, we launched into total Green Day immersion. We came out on the other side, in love with this bighearted rebel.

We asked Adrienne to give us any quotes, poems, lyrics, symbols—anything important to Billie Joe—and she told us about a quote that has become part of their life: "Be silently drawn." This thought became the centerpiece for the entire Airstream, the first thing you see when you walk in the door. We combined elements that worked for him: a little Zen, a little rock star, a little surf shack, and a little retro. We wanted this to be the most streamlined trailer we'd ever done, with vintage reclaimed wood flooring and a 150-year-old Indian temple piece for the bed nook. We MacGyvered our own country-girl surfboard holders out of leather straps on the wall and made a travel-worthy table out of a vintage surfboard.

PITSTOP

Billie Joe Armstrong

Silently Drawn

I was on a walk one morning, and I looked down. In the gutter there was a Post-it. It was handwritten and said "Be Silently Drawn." Those words spoke to me. I picked it up and brought it home. I taped it to the wall next to my bed so I could read it every morning when I woke up. Fast-forward ten years later, the Post-it is still on my wall. One day my wife came across a poem by Rumi and it read, "Let yourself be silently drawn by the strange pull of what you really love. It will not lead you astray." It wasn't until that moment that I knew where those words came from and how they subconsciously impacted my life.

JUST INSIDE THE DOOR OF BILLIE JOE'S ZEN SURF SHACK ARE THE WORDS OF RUMI, HIS FAVORITE POET: "BE SILENTLY DRAWN." WE INSTALLED THE WOOD FLOOR FOR AN EARTHY FEEL.

AMIE'S AIRSTREAM

In the middle of all this Airstream mayhem, we somehow found the time to create a gypsy hideaway for my daughter, Indie, and myself. We took a defunct 1978 Airstream Land Yacht and allowed ourselves to use only things we had in the warehouse. I mixed leftover Ralph Lauren Metallic paints for our own unique rose, adding a whole jar of fine-ground glitter. The final effect: a Neverland escape on wheels.

BEFORE

ABOVE ★ THIS AIRSTREAM WAS A LOVE SONG TO MY
TWO-YEAR-OLD DAUGHTER, AND HER WORLD WAS
EVERYTHING PINK AND SPARKLES. THE SOFA WAS
TWENTY BUCKS AT AN AUCTION, GUSSIED UP WITH A
BIT OF FRINGE. THE BOOTH USED TO BE A BED WE
COULD NEVER SELL. *RIGHT* ★ SOMETIMES YOU GOTTA
WORK BEFORE YOU WORK.

MAGIC IN A TIN CAN

CLOCKWISE FROM TOP LEFT ★ NATURALLY WE NEEDED A PINK ZEBRA RUG. ★ THIS AIRSTREAM IS A LAND YACHT, SO I DECOUPAGED THE HEADBOARD WITH VINTAGE MAPS. CASH BAKER AND I SAT FOR DAYS GLUING RHINESTONES ON AN OLD SHIP FROM THE FLEA MARKET. ★ THE TABLETOP IS GUIDED BY THE SPIRITS OF CALAMITY JANE AND ANNIE OAKLEY. ★ A GALVANIZED WATER TROUGH BATHTUB IS PERCHED ON TOP OF THE WHEEL WELL. THE WALL BEHIND IT IS SALVAGED CEILING TINS FRAMED BY OLD SPANISH PORCH COLUMNS.

DIY ⊤⊤⊤⊤ *Small-Space Kitchenette*

Living tiny is pretty grand! Here we've mastered the perfect way to take a whole kitchen and put it in a small space with super hi-fi style. Two-burner cooktop, bar sink, dorm fridge, and a vintage buffet combined with turquoise paint. Perfection! It's fully functional and brings in a cool design aesthetic. Look for old buffets at flea markets or garage sales; the stovetop can be found at almost any RV/camping supply store, and the bar sink at the hardware store.

Before you get started, make sure you have ample room under your chosen buffet for the water and drain lines. We typically have to sacrifice a drawer to allow for this. The countertop also needs to be big enough to accommodate the sink.

1 Use the template that comes with the sink to mark the buffet for sink placement.

2 Using a drill, drill a hole approximately one inch inside the marked space (this will serve as your starting point for step 3).

3 Use a jigsaw to cut around the marked space.

4 Paint the buffet the desired color, sand to distress, and seal with a waterproof polyurethane.

5 Run a bead of plumber's caulking around the hole on the top of the buffet.

6 Place the sink in the hole with the included clips. For this particular project, we also secured the sink with stainless-steel screws. Tweak instructions as needed. Every project is unique.

7 Hook up the water connections and drain.

8 To insert the dorm fridge, cut out the middle of the buffet with a saw. (Supports may be needed if this step requires cutting off center legs.)

9 Good work! You're practically a plumber and a carpenter now.

The
FLEA
MARKET

WHEREVER YOU GO FOR THE REST OF YOUR LIFE, IT STAYS WITH YOU . . . A MOVEABLE FEAST.

—ERNEST HEMINGWAY

Trucks and trailers bursting with architectural wonders, antiques, and boxes of kitsch. Funky ladies in cowgirl boots drinking beer and remembering their rebellious sides. Aging hippies with ponytails and wrinkles talking about how they found religion and left Wall Street, taking to the roads with junk to sell. The Coffee Bug guy collecting tips in a jar labeled SLOW BOAT TO TAHITI.

The flea market is sacred to us. A place that lives and breathes. It moves in and out of time, continually changing, from one hour to the next, offering all the things you don't know you need. People come, people go. It's dynamic. It's diverse. It's uncharted territory, where we can be Thelma and Louise and Indiana Jones all at the same time.

No one ever said, "Sure, start a business out of the flea market, in the dirt and the grime and the grit." But that's what we did. Part accidentally, and part full throttle, chasing down a dream. For almost twenty years, the flea market has been our business school, our safe place, our wild place, our inspiration, our salvation. Our *moveable feast*.

"WELL, WE'RE NOT IN THE MIDDLE OF NOWHERE, BUT WE CAN SEE IT FROM HERE."

—LOUISE IN *THELMA & LOUISE*

CHAPTER 6

After almost fifteen years of crisscrossing the country, our journey kept leading us back to Round Top, Texas. Population 90. As they say, you can take the girl out of the country but you can't take the country out of the girl.

Round Top is where we belong. It's where we decided our gypsy souls could finally settle down. In Round Top, they say there is a certain magic that weaves its way through your heart when you're here. And we believe it's true. You feel it, whether you're just passing through for the day or staying a few nights. There's a sweet enchantment atop the pastures in the early morning as the cows graze, and a thick sparkle in the stars at night as the coyotes howl. There are more trees than parking spaces and more pastures than asphalt. Things are still done on a handshake. There's one stoplight and thousands of bluebonnets. You can still buy on credit at the local mercantile, and your mail finds its way to you even if the sender forgot to put the street address.

But twice a year, the tiny town of Round Top, Texas, explodes into the largest flea market in the nation. Over that week, this sleepy little town transforms from population 90 to more than 150,000.

Texas Antiques Week is known to junkers and designers far and wide. The flea market capital of the universe. The Super Bowl of junk. The biannual migration to the cow pastures of Round Top is like Christmas morning to us. The sights. The sounds. The characters. The energy. It is like lightning in a bottle, alive and full of dynamic, magnetic energy.

We heard legends and lore of Texas Antiques Week, but we never imagined the true mother lode junk Mecca that awaited us there.

THE STEPS AT THE LOCAL LIBRARY.

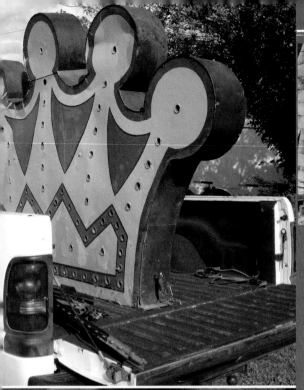

PITSTOP

Matt White

We're All Gypsies

Three thirty AM, the alarm goes off in New Jersey. Then there's a two-hour ride to the airport while half asleep, two hours of airport madness, and a four-hour flight to Texas to pack a tractor trailer. The next twenty-four hours are hell. Loading junk, eating crappy fast food, and living from a backpack. Then you're dragging tail, flying two thousand miles to Brimfield Antique Show to load out in crazy weather, sleeping on the couches you're trying to sell, and staying warm under packing blankets you hope are cleaner than you. That's the life you lead in this bizarre world of junk. The road has taken me to India, China, Africa, Europe, Australia, and all over America many times over—it's a drug. It's what keeps us going. Adventures around the next bend, junk to be bought and sold, life to be lived. You need to be moving constantly. It's unlike any other biz. It's a tough business. But there's none other I'd choose.

The auctioneer at a farm sale once said to me, "Sooo ya wanna be an antique dealer, do ya, kid?" That was thirty-two years ago, and I wouldn't trade a second. That day I bought strawberry picking trays for a quarter and sold them on the way home for ten bucks—hook, line, and sinker—it had me.

FLEA MARKET FIELD GUIDE

Have no fear, junkin' rookies! No need to pull all-nighters for our junkology course. Save that precious energy for the flea market!

JUNKIN' RULE 1
Love it, buy it!

Remember, old stuff is, well, it's *old*. So it may not be perfect, but if it's a piece you truly love, your home and heart will find a place for it. Chipped, cracked, threadbare, or otherwise imperfect? That only adds character to your collection of flea market flair!

JUNKIN' RULE 2
Come with cash in hand!

Head to the flea market with a good supply of cash. Many junk dealers are cash only, plus you'll need food, drinks, and the occasional cold beer.

JUNKIN' RULE 3
Don't be shy! (But be nice.)

Don't be afraid to ask a dealer if the price marked is their lowest price, but don't haggle over a few dollars. Be careful not to negotiate a price in an abrasive manner: You'll only insult the dealer and end up missing the chance at a fab piece. Basically, if you think the price is fair, just let it ride. You don't *always* have to get it cheaper than the asking price to be going home with an amazing deal.

JUNKIN' RULE 4
Be a die-hard!

Relentless searching sometimes ends with the grandest find of the day. We're not lucky; we're persistent. This is not the mall. You won't find exactly what you're looking for every single time. Remember the thrill of the hunt? Well, without the *hunt* part, there ain't no thrill. Enjoy the process, even when you don't find the diamond in the dust. Tomorrow is another day.

JUNKIN' RULE 5
Listen and learn!

Flea markets are the best place on the planet to learn about antiques, vintage art, and the history of unique treasures, not to mention vendors who know all the best secrets on the coolest haunts and jaunts. So keep those ears to the ground and learn, learn, learn!

JUNKIN' RULE 6
Gear up!

Make like a Boy Scout and be prepared! Here are a few junkin' survival necessities:

- ★ HAT AND SUNGLASSES
- ★ SUNSCREEN
- ★ COMFORTABLE CLOTHES AND SHOES (PREPARE FOR ANY TYPE OF WEATHER)
- ★ YOUR BIGGEST AUTOMOBILE, TRUCK, VAN, U-HAUL, OR SUV
- ★ A TARP, BUNGEE CORDS, AND ROPES TO PROTECT AND TIE DOWN ANY LARGE PURCHASES
- ★ A COOLER WITH WATER AND OTHER FAVORITE BEVERAGES
- ★ A TAPE MEASURE
- ★ PAINT CHIPS, FABRIC SWATCHES, AND ANY VITAL MEASUREMENTS FOR THE PIECES YOU ARE HUNTING

JUNKIN' RULE 7
Live the day!

In the end, junkin' is about the search, the discovery, and the excitement you feel when you find the perfect piece for your pad. Savor the thrill of the hunt. Look around and take in the eccentricities in all the great junk around you. Laugh with your friends and learn something new from a seasoned junk dealer.

JUNKIN' RULE 8
Get to know the vendors.

Flea market folks all have a great story to tell, which gives your flea market find an even cooler story. If you're a reseller, introduce yourself and let the vendor know. They often have "dealer" pricing.

JUNKIN' RULE 9
Know when to hold 'em and know when to fold 'em.

Keep that poker face! Junkers are smart, so don't imagine you'll put something over on them, but play it cool, curb your enthusiasm, and start by asking, "What's your best price?" Civilized junking is about striking a win-win deal, not haggling.

JUNKIN' RULE 10
Hang in there till the bitter end.

Another reason it pays to be a die-hard: a lot of the greatest deals happen in the final hours. Circle back. You might get lucky on an item you tried to negotiate earlier. Besides, you don't want to miss the flea market at night. The stars above, tents lined up on the moonlit horizon, the faint sound of music in the distance, the smell of campfires in the air. And little pockets of junkers everywhere, sitting around discussing everything from politics to the big sale of the day, hypothesizing on the ups and downs of the flea market like it's the stock market, which in many ways it is. It ebbs and flows—up and down, back and forth—directly proportional to the weather, gas prices, and whether it's an election year.

Inside the Junk Gypsy Tent

The phrase "true north" conjures an image of a compass, a map, and cardinal directions, but it also has a deeper meaning. In his book *True North*, Harvard professor Bill George says: "It is your orienting point—your fixed point in a spinning world—that helps you stay on track." I and thousands of other people, from music royalty to the everyday mom with a camera, take time twice a year to visit, shop, laugh, ooh and aah, and get inspired, finding our true north by way of Texas Antiques Week. In the Junk Gypsy tent, you see more than a bunch of cool, old stuff for sale; you see a purposeful symmetry of colors, vintage artifacts, foliage, and more. Mind you—this is in the middle of a field!

—APRIL PIZANA

THIS AIN'T THE MALL.
THERE'RE WOOD
SHAVINGS ON THE
GROUND AND TEXAS
BEER ON TAP.

ABOVE ★ OH, THE MEMORIES THIS COUNTER HOLDS! WE CREATED THE ARCH BY ATTACHING OLD PORCH COLUMNS, AND IT'S SEEN MANY A FLEA MARKET, ALWAYS DECKED OUT IN A DIFFERENT THEME. HERE IT'S COVERED IN CONCERT POSTERS, TOPPED OFF WITH AN ELECTRIC GUITAR AND GIANT OLD WINGS. *OPPOSITE, CLOCKWISE FROM TOP LEFT* ★ AFTER TEN DAYS OF SETUP, WE'RE FINALLY READY TO OPEN OUR DOORS—OR OUR TENT FLAPS. ★ THE JUXTAPOSITION OF ALL THINGS GYPSY: SALVAGED DOORS AND STATUES, A BIRDCAGE CHANDELIER, AND AN ASSORTMENT OF FUN, FLUFFY PILLOWS. ★ NEON AND OLD LACE SET OFF A VINTAGE BEDSTEAD.

AMERICANA

Americana is one of our favorite ways to decorate. We love Old Glory and all things starry and striped, but Americana is more than red, white, and blue. It's evocative and nostalgic: red-tufted chesterfields; marching-band hats with fluffy, feathery red plumes; vintage band jackets; and gold chandeliers. If it speaks to your sense of history and makes you feel like singing "This Land Is Your Land"—that's Americana.

DIY 𝀇𝀇𝀇𝀇 Piano Table

"Well, it's nine o'clock on a Saturday . . ."

This project requires a little more elbow grease than some, but it's well worth it in the end. We find high-mileage pianos for sale all the time, and they're often really cheap or even free because of their size. We promise it'll be the coolest thing in your pad!

1 Clean the keyboard and measure to determine the size of your table.

2 Build a shadowbox concept frame with a floor to house the keyboard. We used salvaged wood here, but new wood can also be used.

3 Attach legs to the bottom of the frame. We salvaged these legs, but new spindles from the lumberyard would work perfectly.

4 Top it off with glass or Plexiglas, whichever you prefer. Local home improvement stores can often cut these to size. Do not try to cut on your own.

SAFETY TIP: IF YOU USE GLASS, CHOOSE SAFETY GLASS TO PREVENT BREAKAGE UNDER STRESS.

"THE ROAD GOES ON FOREVER AND THE PARTY NEVER ENDS."
—ROBERT EARL KEEN

CHAPTER 7

No one's ever accused us of being event planners. We aren't members of the Pinterest party revolution. We don't throw big-dollar, photo-worthy birthday parties for our kids or dive into the high school reunion gala committee. Ironically, though we've been involved in some pretty epic parties, celebrity weddings, and backstage events.

To us, a party is more about the electric energy of the event. It's about the ease of the moment. It's about creating an environment that lets the guests feel less like guests and more like kindred spirits. It's about less effort and more comfort. And sometimes all it takes is an old record player and your favorite vinyls to release the inner party animal.

The JG Junk-O-Rama Prom is a great example of what we're talking about. What started as a simple ode to the forgotten prom dress magically took a life of its own one night at the flea market. During Texas Antiques Week several years ago, we noticed the glory and beauty of reclaimed vintage prom dresses. It seemed almost tragic that these magnificent piles of taffeta and lace—often handmade works of art—were now destined for the dump. We decided it was up to us to pay tribute to these faded beauties by hosting our own little prom a few nights later. We scavenged the grounds, scooped up vintage dresses throughout the week, and all danced under the stars that one night.

There were a handful of customers and several junkers at that first Junk-O-Rama Prom. We drank sangria, took pictures, practically danced holes in our boots, and had lots of laughs, completely oblivious to the fact that the Junk-O-Rama Prom would soon become a legendary twice-yearly event.

For one breathtaking evening under the big ol' southern stars, with folks of all ages and walks of life in attendance, we stir up memories by the light of the moon. The whole shindig takes place at our tent, which is basically a transformed Texas cow pasture. The band plays on a makeshift stage adorned with our latest, greatest flea market finds and a million and one twinkling lights. Glittery chandeliers hang from the trees.

The Junk-O-Rama Prom has become a cultural crossroads of sights and sounds and people. And, we firmly believe, for a brilliant moment, it's the happiest place on Earth. To truly understand what it's like, you need to be there. Next best thing: Go to Spotify and listen to Robert Earl Keen's "The Road Goes On Forever."

Seriously. Do that right now. We'll wait.

DIY 🔨 *Photo Booth*

The original outhouse from the Zapp Hall grounds functions as our official photo booth, retrofitted in true Junk Gypsy fashion with posh, tattered velvet curtains and old oil paintings. Construct your own photo booth from old doors. Decorate with anything salvage you can find—an awning, corbels, old signs—and don't forget bunting and a chandelier for the finishing touch.

OVER-THE-TOP PROM COSTUME DIY GENIUS

Through the years, amid the glitter and the grit, the debutantes and the dirt, the most entertaining aspect of the Junk-O-Rama Prom is the outrageous creativity of the costumes. Prom guests show up wearing bedazzled lampshades as hats, glittered deer antlers as crowns, newspaper dresses, and full-on Elvis regalia—the die-hard Junk-O-Rama Prom devotees never cease to amaze, and the magic never stops.

CLOCKWISE FROM TOP LEFT ★ THIS BELT BUCKLE WAS CONCOCTED FROM BUTTONS, BOTTLE CAPS, AND COSTUME JEWELRY ALL SERVED UP ON A SILVER PLATTER. ★ OUR FRIEND KACI SHOWS HOW YOU CAN EMBELLISH A HAT IN VINTAGE PROM STYLE! ★ THIS JUNK QUEEN CREATED HER HEADDRESS FROM AN UPSIDE-DOWN COLANDER, DISCARDED BABY DOLL ARMS, CHRISTMAS ORNAMENTS, FLOWERS, AND FLAWLESS TIMING. ★ WITH DISCARDED LAMPSHADES, A LITTLE BIT OF HOT GLUE, AND A LOT OF CREATIVITY, THESE SHADY LADIES STOLE THE SHOW.

DIY 🔨 *Glitter Shaker*

We believe glitter is a color of the rainbow. Nothing—we repeat, nothing—is simpler to make than this glitter shaker, and like salt and pepper shakers, it makes life easier. Just be sure you don't sprinkle it on your eggs. Might be a little crunchy. Although we have considered glitter for breakfast.

1 Unscrew the lid off your trusty mason jar and hold it firmly on a flat surface.

2 Using a hammer and a tenpenny-type nail, tap holes into the lid.

3 Fill the jar with glitter.

4 Now consider yourself armed and dangerous and ready to glitter the world!

IMPORTANT SAFETY TIP:
USE A LOW-WATTAGE
LIGHTBULB TO AVOID A
FIRE HAZARD.

DIY ⚒ *Glitter Feather Chandelier*

We have a small problem called "lampshade boredom blues." Thankfully, there is a cure! Just use the frame from an old ribbed lampshade, add glitter and feathers, and you've got the perfect boho style for your space! Use it on a lamp or hang it from a ten-dollar light cord.

1 Scrounge up a nice ribbed lampshade. If it still has the fabric on it, strip that off, leaving the metal frame.

2 Spray the tips of the feathers with spray paint. We love the look of gold paint with gold glitter on white feathers, but you should be able to find just about any color your little heart desires.

3 While the paint is still wet, sprinkle with glitter. (This is the perfect time to crack out that handy-dandy glitter shaker you just made.)

4 Tie the feathers to the lampshade frame using monofilament.

5 Attach the lampshade to your favorite lamp or use a ten-dollar light cord and hang it from the ceiling or a bracket.

6 Turn on the lamp and bask in the glow of your artsy accomplishment!

SADIE ROBERTSON'S SWEET 16

When the Ducks called, we answered, decorating a Sweet 16 party for Sadie Robertson, who's a star in her own right as a *Dancing with the Stars* runner-up and Internet sensation. This soiree called for loads of glitter, disco balls, and a graffiti couch. The theme: Redneck Red Carpet. Our mission (as stated by Sadie): "The most *amazing* party that has ever happened in the world." So no pressure.

PITSTOP

Sadie Robertson

Birthday Girl

The Junk Gypsies know how to throw a party! They make you feel special and make every little touch so personal to you. It was the best day of my life. Just knowing how big their hearts are—to come and decorate the coolest tent ever—it meant the world to me. It was a day I will cherish forever. I can't wait to tell my kids about it one day!

CLOCKWISE FROM TOP LEFT ★ GLITTERY DUCK DECOYS CREATE A ONE-OF-A-KIND CHANDELIER. ★ CROWN PRINCESS OF THE REDNECK RED CARPET. ★ MINGLE-FRIENDLY CONVERSATION NOOKS. ★ THIS TUFTED VELVET HEADBOARD IS A TRUE USE-WHAT-YOU-GOT MOMENT. IT'S BROUGHT DRAMA AND COLOR TO SEVERAL EVENTS. HERE IT'S A GREAT PHOTO BACKGROUND.

DIY ⚒ *Graffiti Sofa*

This is the perfect addition to any party: It's lots of fun for guests and a great way for the guest of honor to remember the occasion for years to come. You can always find old upholstered furniture at secondhand stores or on the side of the road on big-trash day for free!

1 Rescue a secondhand, upholstered sofa or chair from a yard sale, thrift store, or curb.

2 Paint with at least two coats of water-based paint. White paint works best. We used glossy, but any finish is just fine. Be sure to cover the entire sofa with paint. You need a clean canvas.

3 Grab Sharpies, paint pens, and markers and release your inner graffiti artist!

"CLOTHES AREN'T GOING TO CHANGE THE WORLD; THE WOMEN WHO WEAR THEM WILL."

—ANNE KLEIN

IF WILLIE & JANIS HAD A LOVE CHILD

CHAPTER 8

There once was a time we both "dressed for success," as you might say. We had pencil skirts, button-down shirts, panty hose (Heaven have mercy!) and yes, even heels. We had *an iron*. We had khaki slacks. With pleats. In the "What was I thinking?" style category, pleats rank right up there with layering socks. Meg Ryan is the only person on God's green earth who makes pleats look good.

We both lasted about three years imprisoned in these inhumane conditions before we finally came to realize two essential truths: 1) Our trying to conform to typical office dress codes was a lost cause. And 2) panty hose are the province of Lucifer.

The first rule of order when we fled our fashion-entrapped lives and jumped on the Junk Gypsy karma train was to toss those panty hose, irons, and khakis out the window. You're welcome. Don't nobody need to be seeing either one of us in a pair of panty hose. Or khakis, for that matter. Once we'd returned to our natural state of style (jeans), our spirits were uninhibited and our creativity was freed like a wayward antelope to its natural habitat.

The universe rejoiced.

Somebody say amen and put on the denim.

When we were kids, we had a huge barrel of dress-up clothes. Every time Mom went to a garage sale, flea market, or thrift store, she'd bring back a rhinestone-clad disco dress, Asian robe, polyester suit, platform shoes, elbow-length gloves, or wigs of all colors to add to this barrel full of possibilities. In hindsight, this barrel was a magic time machine, a portal to "dream big, my child," a foundation for our love of unique, individual style.

Our "new school clothes" shopping trips entailed going to all of our favorite resale shops, finding things we never knew we needed. For us, the fun and mystery of shopping at a thrift store far outweighed the humdrum predictability of the shopping mall.

From the fringe-laden, turquoise-studded frontier to ripped jeans and old T-shirts, our personal style—like our decorating style—is eclectic and adheres to very few conventional rules. It's uncomplicated, irreverent, and free-spirited, inspired by some of history's fashion trailblazers, like Jimi Hendrix, Ralph Lauren, and Stevie Nicks.

Junk Gypsy style combines everything we love—everything we appreciate, everything that has soul—with fringe, crushed velvet, ripped-up denim, sequins, vintage concert tees, turquoise, and tooled western belts.

It's hippie and boho.

It's Texas.

It's rock 'n' roll rebel meets Wild West outlaw.

It's Elizabethan poet meets Sgt. Pepper.

It's us.

WHAT'S IN THE JUNK GYPSY TRAVEL BAG?

OUR UNIFORM IS PRETTY MUCH THE SAME, WHETHER WE'RE IN NEW YORK TO APPEAR ON THE *TODAY* SHOW OR ON THE ROAD IN SEARCH OF ROADSIDE TREASURES. A FEW THINGS WE WON'T LEAVE HOME WITHOUT:

★ RIPPED-UP, WORN-OUT BLUE JEANS

★ WORK GLOVES

★ OLD PEARL-SNAP WESTERN SHIRTS

★ FRINGED LEATHER JACKETS

★ MILITARY JACKETS

★ TURQUOISE JEWELRY

★ VINTAGE JEWELRY

★ SCUFFED-UP BOOTS

★ WRINKLED TEES (EXTRA POINTS FOR OLD CONCERT TEES)

★ VINTAGE TOOLED LEATHER BELTS AND SILVER BUCKLES

★ FRINGED LEATHER PURSES

BONUS STEP FOR OVERACHIEVERS: USE A SEAM RIPPER TO RIP OUT THE BOTTOM SEAM FOR ADDED EFFECT.

DIY ⚒ *Distressing Jeans*

Fifteen years ago, we decided new jeans were just too . . . well, *new*. We wanted them to have that secondhand look, that *worked-in* look, that "these jeans have a story to tell" look. So we did what any self-respecting gypsy would do: We destructed them. Take a perfectly good pair of blue jeans, grab a pair of scissors, and get ready to become a rock star.

1 Put your jeans on and look in the mirror.

2 Use a Sharpie to mark where your kneecaps are on both legs of your jeans.

3 Ready to do some damage? Lay the jeans flat on a solid surface.

4 Slide a small piece of cardboard inside the pant leg and up to the target area of destruction.

5 With scissors flayed out, blade horizontal, scrape back and forth, cutting through the denim. Easy there, Edward Scissorhands! Use caution that you don't cut yourself instead of the jeans. A box cutter can also be used instead of scissors if you have one handy. It's a little safer and still gets the job done.

6 Keep scraping back and forth until you've created a large hole almost the width of the jean leg.

7 Repeat this process on a pocket or wherever you want to have additional distressing.

8 Wash and dry the jeans, pair them with your favorite tee and some well-worn boots.

9 Congratulations. You're officially a rock star.

OUR FIRST TEE DESIGN

Amie's mind is like a glittery tumbleweed: It sometimes touches ground, but usually it spins along a few feet in the air. With no formal training in graphic design, she created our first tee by gathering elements from a few of her favorite things: a vintage image of cowgirls, an old frame from a flea market photo album, and a Laurel Thatcher Ulrich quote she'd had stuck to her mirror since college: "Well-behaved women rarely make history."

When we started to unpack the tees at Texas Antiques Week, those boxes got mobbed like a Macy's one-day sale. Shoppers rifled the neatly folded, freshly printed tees faster than we could unpack 'em. Before the show even started, we'd sold almost every single one, including the shirts off our backs. Literally! A lady actually pleaded with us to hand over the shirts we'd been wearing for three days. And we're talking about three *flea market* days. It's like dog years. One day at the flea market produces as much dirt and sweat as three weeks of normal life.

Women connected with this tee. They *got* it. They wanted to wear something that spoke to them— and spoke their mind. We knew immediately: We had to make more tees! And we had to pour that same passion and soul into each one.

MAMA TRIED

In 2005, as a tribute to Merle Haggard, Miranda wore our "Mama Tried" tank in her video for "Kerosene." It went on to become her first Top 20 country hit, marking a pivotal point for us all. The tank represented more than just a tank for her; it was a statement of who she is. The video was a moment in her career that defined her and introduced Miranda Lambert to the world in a way no one had seen her before.

PITSTOP
MIRANDA LAMBERT

Go Big, Be Bold

These amazing people make me proud to be from Texas. Their style and spunk inspire me every day. They're never afraid to go big. And be bold. They're about empowering women, and being fearless, and embracing yourself. Most important, they value family and believing in your roots. I'm blessed to call them my friends.

DIY 👕👕 T-shirt Curtains

Curtains made of tees are the best idea ever for honoring your most cherished tees and the memories that go with them—the good, the bad, and the glorious—and for rehabbing those crop tops that don't fit anymore. Mixing and matching tees with vintage fabrics lends stability, makes it easier to sew, and creates a great patchwork effect. Perfect for any room.

1 Cut squares of fabric and tees. We typically do twelve-inch or ten-inch squares. It helps if the tees are all approximately the same size.

2 Sew the squares together, alternating tees and fabric, to create long strips that are the height of your window plus a little.

3 Repeat step 2 as many times as you need to cover the width of your window or door.

4 Sew the long strips together until the correct size is reached.

BONUS STEP FOR OVERACHIEVERS: ADD A LINER TO YOUR PANEL. WE USED GAUZE HERE, BUT A WASHED BEDSHEET WORKS GREAT. TO PREVENT PUCKERING, SEW THE LINER AT THE TOP ONLY.

DAYDREAM BELIEVER

Through a series of fortunate events, PBteen walked through our doors in 2014, and thus began our foray into designing for teens. It was pretty much a dream gig, since we don't believe in acting like grown-ups, or dressing like them, or decorating like them. We know that teens want to make their space a true reflection of who they are, and that is never just one thing. So we set out to give them something fierce *and* dreamy. Rebellious *and* sweet. It's a beautiful hodgepodge of our style philosophy applied to decor. Faded denim and vintage lace. Old concert tees and eyelet skirts. It's us. It's you. It's *personal*.

CLOCKWISE FROM TOP LEFT ★ WE LOVE THE WAY THIS CAST-IRON, VINTAGE-INSPIRED BED LOOKS WITH COUNTRY BLOOMS AND SERAPE PATTERN SHAMS. ★ OUR THEME FOR THIS ROOM WAS "DREAM BIG!" WE INCORPORATED COMPASSES, MAPS, GLITTER DREAMER LETTERS, AND A CRYSTAL-CLAD PIRATE SHIP, INSPIRED BY THE SHIP CHANDELIER AT AMIE'S HOUSE. ★ THE ONLY THING BETTER THAN A CHESTERFIELD SOFA IS A STONEWASHED-DENIM CHESTERFIELD SOFA—SO WE DESIGNED ONE. THE HEART WITH WINGS IS A JG MAINSTAY AND ENDED UP BEING ONE OF THE MOST POPULAR ITEMS IN THE LINE. ★ WE WORKED HARD TO CAPTURE THE SPIRIT OF JUNK GYPSY, AS SEEN IN OUR PILLOW COLLECTION.

173

#Don'tWearHeels

We live, work, and play in our boots. Boots are more than just another accessory. Boots are a girl's best friend. They're part of your spirit. Memories made. New paths forged. They tell your story—where you've been and where there is yet to go.

PITSTOP

Amy "Archie" Allen

What Fringe Hath Brought Together...

Do you ever look back and think, "That was a defining moment"? I'm not talking about the obvious big, monumental events here; I'm talking about a chance meeting on a Tuesday night in a smoky blues bar on the third floor of a century-old building in Bryan, Texas. You had to climb creaky, narrow stairs covered in avocado-green shag carpet to reach this place filled with leather sofas and signed headshots of blues singers. It was my favorite place when I was in college, but on this particular night, something out of the ordinary caught my attention.

A girl walked past me, and swaying on her shoulder was the most beautiful buckskin fringe bag I'd ever seen. I mean gorgeous. I had a fringe purse too: a hand-me-down from my mom, which for some reason had four of my baby teeth in a little pocket on the side. This girl's bag was way cooler than mine. I had to know who owned this masterpiece.

The girl and the purse disappeared into the bathroom. I followed, trying to play it cool.

"I love your purse. Love it! I followed you in here so I could tell you that."

"Thank you," she said, unfazed by the accidental creepiness. "I like yours too. I'm Amie. Where are you from?"

My accent had already stolen the show. She knew I was from East Texas. We actually grew up close to each other. Between that and our mutual love of fringe and old blues bars, we hit it off.

A few months later, Amie called to see if I'd be interested in modeling for an upcoming photo shoot. I remember pacing. Barefoot. Nervous. But Amie seemed confident that I'd be just fine. So I was in.

In the JG warehouse the day of the first shoot there was a huge table covered in turquoise jewelry, hats, boots, jackets, and fringe. Lots of fringe. A crazy collaboration of everything I loved. I was hooked. I had to be a part of this world somehow. I did a few more photo shoots, and then they hired me to help in the warehouse part-time. After college, I moved to Argentina for a while and then roamed around Texas, trying to figure out what to do next. When Amie and Jolie offered me a full-time job, I didn't even have to think about it. I took that big ol' leap of faith.

Junk Gypsy had been a part of my life for four years and felt like a big part of *me* from the first time I saw it—"it" being the magic, an aura that makes people feel like they're part of something special—not just as a customer, but part of the lifestyle. So many people say, "I never knew until now, but I'm a Junk Gypsy."

Amie and Jolie treat their customers like family, laugh with them, cry with them, and are truly thankful for them. They're thankful for the stories of how JG has changed lives, stories of inspiration, hope, and having the courage to follow their dreams because of Junk Gypsy. That's what I love most: the magic. JG is a brand people love, but harder to define—and bigger than

the love for a turquoise dresser or a vintage squash blossom necklace, or even an amazing fringe purse—is the way JG empowers people and sets them free. What is life if you aren't doing what you love? What is life if you aren't happy? Dream big dreams. Hell, dream huge dreams! Junk Gypsy evokes something special—something big—in people from two to ninety-two.

When I started my full-time job at Junk Gypsy I was an inexperienced kid, but I loved working every day in a place that made people feel happy and inspired. If something came up, we figured it out together. And we still do. Looking back on that Tuesday night, I would have never thought that a chance meeting and a mutual love of fringe would lead me here. But I'm so glad it did.

FRINGE

If loving fringe is wrong,
we don't want to be right.
Period. End of story.

HOME

NO ONE APPRECIATES HOME MORE THAN A WANDERER.

Although we have a very real love affair with the road, there's nothing we love more than coming home.

Home is where your mom is. Home is family. Home is roots. Home is gratitude.

Home is the place where all your adventures come together like stars spinning in the cosmos, forming one pristine constellation.

The constellation of your life.

Our deep roots and deep love of family connect us to home in a fierce and fiery way. You know that feeling you get when you put on your favorite pair of old beat-up blue jeans? The ones that are threadbare and faded? That's how home should feel. It should be your cozy place. Your escape. There shouldn't be any rules.

"I ain't rich, but Lord I'm free."

—GEORGE STRAIT, "AMARILLO BY MORNING"

SO GOD MADE A FARMHOUSE

CHAPTER 9

The country. Wide-open spaces that seem to go on forever and ever.

The nothingness that really is everything.

American farmland. Windmills. Hay bales. Tractors. Ponds.

Uncomplicated. Unspoiled. Land as God made it.

Land serving man and man serving land in a symbiotic relationship of give-and-take. The backbone on which the country was founded—by people who found joy in simple things and didn't live in a disposable world.

To us the farmhouse style hearkens back to those days. Even though we live in farmhouses where we have Wi-Fi and a color TV, we still believe in the power of the farm.

There's this little thing we call "granny economics." It's the idea of using what you have instead of buying something new. The belief that new isn't always better. Like how our granny used the same worn-out tin can for more than fifty years to cut biscuits instead of buying an actual biscuit cutter. Because, to her, that worn-out can worked fine, so why buy a new one?

If it ain't broke, don't fix it.

FARMHOUSE STYLE

Charm meets function. Hard meets soft. Soothing neutrals meet pops of vibrant color. Above all else, farmhouse style is about that buttermilk-biscuit feeling that tells you you're home.

186

HOME

CLOCKWISE FROM TOP LEFT ★
MISMATCHED OLD SIGN LETTERS BRING
CHARM TO MODERN CONVENIENCE. ★
JOLIE AND CASH BAKER OUTSIDE THEIR
HOMEMADE CHICKEN COOP, COMPLETE
WITH CHANDELIER AND ROOSTER
OIL PAINTING THAT KEEPS THE HENS
MOTIVATED. ★ WE CONVERTED A
CENTURY-OLD TEXAS WINDMILL TO AN
EIGHT-FOOT CEILING FAN FOR JOLIE'S
LIVING ROOM. THIS IS SERIOUSLY THE
BIGGEST CEILING FAN KNOWN TO
MANKIND AND ONE OF THE BIGGEST
DIYS WE'VE EVER TACKLED.

AN OLD BARN GATE MOUNTED TO THE WALL WITH VINTAGE BARN DOOR
HARDWARE MAKES THE PERFECT RUSTIC HEADBOARD. ★ DON'T
SEQUESTER THOSE ACCESSORIES IN A CLOSET. IN OUR WORLD, STASHED
UNDER AN OLD FARM BENCH WITH CHIPPY PAINT, BOOTS MAKE GREAT
DECOR. APPLY AS NEEDED TO YOUR JEWELRY, BELTS, AND HATS. ★
ANOTHER WAY TO USE AN OLD GATE. THIS PIECE OF OLD FENCING
BEAUTIFULLY BACKDROPS A GEORGIA O'KEEFFE—STYLE COW SKULL.

Hey good-Lookin'
Whatcha got Cookin'?
Blue Plate Special
Biscuits & gravy 25¢
iced tea
lemon-ade
coffee
FLOUR

DIY 🔨🔨🔨 Chalkboard Pantry Door

The absolute easiest way to disguise a basic hollow-core door: just add chalkboard paint. This door is perfect for any room, but we really love it as a pantry. Grab sliding hardware at your local farm supply store.

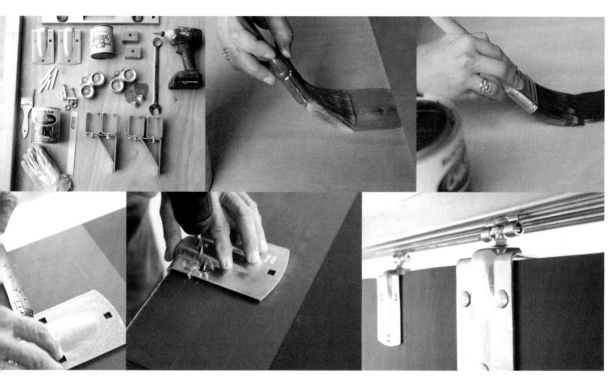

1 Prime and then paint the hollow core door with chalkboard paint according to the instructions on the can.

2 Following the package instructions, mount box rail track on your wall.

3 Attach box rail hangers to door using bolts included in the set. Be sure you measure so they are equal distance from the edge of the door. We placed ours about five inches from the edge. (Pro tip: We used painter's tape to protect the door from scratches while measuring the hardware. Just don't forget to remove tape before bolting down the hangers!)

4 Slide your door into the rail track. You'll need to attach a stopper to the end of the rail to keep your door from derailing. We used the one that came with the kit.

PROJECT *Farmhouse Kitchen*

While we were filming the first season of our HGTV show, we did a romantic cowgirl bedroom for our friend Kelley Keen. She's the quintessential Texas woman: pearls and leather, tough but tender. In season three, we tackled her kitchen, which embodies all the functional charm of farmhouse style.

BEFORE

LEFT ★ KELLEY'S DARK CAVE OF A KITCHEN WAS A FLASHBACK TO THE 1970S AND DIDN'T FIT HER PERSONALITY AT ALL. *FAR LEFT* ★ WE KNOCKED OUT HALF THE WALL FOR AN OPEN-CONCEPT FEEL AND BROUGHT IN THIS OLD COLUMN FOR SUPPORT AND ARCHITECTURAL INTEREST. STAINLESS-STEEL COUNTERTOPS BRING IN CLEAN LINES AND AN INDUSTRIAL VIBE. *ABOVE* ★ FARMHOUSE MEETS GLAM: THIS WAGON-WHEEL-AND-MASON-JAR CHANDELIER DRIPPING WITH CRYSTALS PERFECTLY SUMS UP KELLEY'S PERSONAL STYLE.

APRICOT NUT BREAD

cup dried apricots
cup sugar
T. shortening
egg, well-beaten
cup orange juice
cup sugar

2 cups sifted flour
2 tsp. baking powder
½ cup chopped nuts
1 tsp. salt
½ tsp. soda

Cook apricots for 20 minutes, cream the one cup sugar, shortening, and egg well. Stir in orange juice mixed with the cup sugar. Add dry ingredients and blend well. Drain apricots and stir into batter with nuts.

Bake in greased and floured 8x5x3 loaf pan about 375° for about 45 minutes. Makes two loaves. Freezes well.

Cecile Tyler

DIY 🔨 *Recipe Card Decoupage*

There's a beautiful soul behind an old recipe card. The handwritten ingredients, the stains on the card, the worn edges. These cards have a story to tell. They are part of your story. Part of your ancestry. So why not make them part of your decor? You can do this really simple decoupage project for under five dollars.

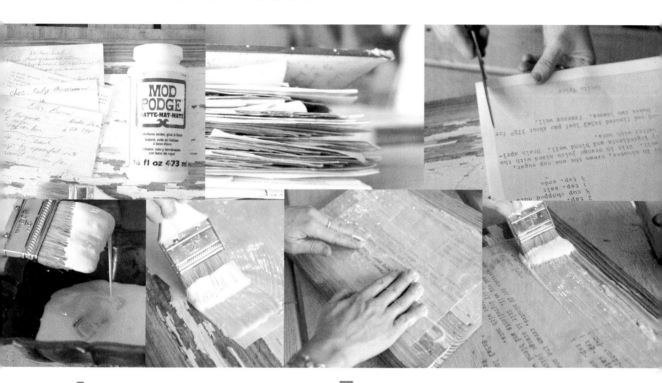

1 Prepare the wood surface by cleaning off excess chippy paint and/or dirt.

2 Make a photocopy of the recipe card.

3 Using scissors, trim excess white space from the copy.

4 Liberally apply Mod Podge to the back of the recipe card and place on the board.

5 Using your hands or a straight edge, gently smooth out the card, pushing out excess Mod Podge and bubbles.

6 Brush Mod Podge on top of the card.

7 Smooth again. Very important! You'll have a wrinkly finished product if you don't smooth, smooth, smooth.

8 Drill two holes in the top of the board and thread with a piece of wire for a rustic hanger.

GALVANIZED

In our world, galvanized is the new black—and it goes hand-in-hand with farmhouse style. Buckets, troughs, and tanks are multifunctional and practical—the perfect marriage of industrial and farmhouse design.

LEFT ★ A LIVESTOCK WATER TROUGH RETROFITTED WITH SIMPLE OUTDOOR PLUMBING FIXTURES BENEATH A VINTAGE ADVERTISEMENT BECOMES A COWGIRL HOT TUB. PRO TIP: WE DO NOT RECOMMEND LANDSCAPING WITH POISON IVY, AS YOU SEE HERE. ★ A MODERN FARMHOUSE TWIST ON A SHOWER USING GALVANIZED CORRUGATED SHEET METAL. THEY'LL USUALLY CUT AND THREAD PIPES FOR YOU AT YOUR LOCAL HARDWARE STORE.

PROJECT *Rustic Farmhouse Bathroom*

Old sideboards, dressers, and buffets can be repurposed as the perfect lavatory, bringing salvage into your space in a functional way. We found this one at the flea market for under $200, dropped in a sink, and gave it a little paint upgrade. If standard bathtub skirting options just aren't your style, bring in salvaged chippy-peely wood. It brings a "something old" element into a new space, adding farmhouse charm. A few coats of polyurethane preserve the chippy-peely look.

DIY 🔨🔨 Farmhouse Coffee Table

Sick of your Mediterranean coffee table? Turn it around with rustic farmhouse charm. (You can undo this and make it Mediterranean again later, if that suits your fancy.) Have no fear: Most hardware stores will cut the wood to length for you, which makes this project even easier.

1 Lightly sand the coffee table as needed. We like to knock off a little of the "new" paint to give it a distressed look.

2 Measure coffee table for length and width. (Measure twice, cut once!)

3 Cut the appropriate number of wood slats to appropriate lengths.

4 Hammer each slat into place with finishing nails. It's easier if you use a C-clamp to hold wood in place while you're hammering.

BONUS STEP: ADD A COAT OF POLYURETHANE FOR A WATER-RESISTANT SURFACE AND TO PREVENT SPLINTERS.

LOVE SONG TO THE SMALL TOWN

We are small-town girls to the core, raised in Overton, Texas. Our personal Mayberry. Between its single, flashing red light and the almost spiritual football stadium, this little oilfield town nestles in the pine-covered hills of East Texas. The Dairy Queen stands at the edge of town like a beacon in the night, and at the local grocery store, the boys still carry your groceries out to your car, even if it's just a jug of milk. During your lunch break, you can walk from the downtown florist to the post office, visit the public library, and still have time to grab a slice of meringue pie and a cup of coffee with the mayor at the local café.

As teenagers, we rode in the backs of pickup trucks to our parents' pizza place for lunch. Fitting as many kids as possible into the cab and the bed became a bona fide sport. Boys were required to tuck their shirttails in before class, to take their caps off at the door, and to walk a girl to the door after a date. With the sounds of Bon Jovi in the background and the smell of Rave hair spray filling our trucks, we'd cruise Main Street every weekend. The old school auditorium (circa 1932) still stands, with its dusty green velvet curtains and hardwood stage. We stood on that stage for plays, for speeches, for giving blood, for taking school pictures, and for graduating.

There is a rich history that paves the streets of every small town, including our new Mayberry, Round Top, Texas. The sidewalks may roll up come nightfall, but the people who live and die there form the beautiful patchwork quilt that is small-town life.

BELOW ★ LARGE MARGE IN THE ROUND TOP ANNUAL FOURTH OF JULY PARADE. A TRADITION SINCE 1851, IT'S THE LONGEST-RUNNING INDEPENDENCE DAY CELEBRATION WEST OF THE MISSISSIPPI. *TOP RIGHT* ★ WORLD-FAMOUS ROYERS CAFE ON THE SQUARE—SOUTHERN COMFORT FOOD AT ITS FINEST. *BOTTOM RIGHT* ★ KIDS WATCHING THE CHUTE AT THE SHERIFF'S POSSE RANCH RODEO.

"GO OUT FOR ADVENTURE; COME HOME FOR LOVE."

—UNKNOWN

HOME SWEET HOME GYPSY

CHAPTER 10

We've roamed far and wide throughout this book. Now we're bringing it all home to our own houses. Our philosophy is that home decor shouldn't be taken too seriously, because we want our homes to reflect who we are, no one else.

We want things to be fun and interesting, but we want things we can really live with and around. We want a place where you can use Play-Doh or prop up crusty old cowboy boots on the coffee table. We're not afraid of candle drippings or drink rings. We believe all these things help our homes tell a tale of love and family. A tale of history and future. A tale of the American experience. Our homes spin the story we want to live in every day.

We firmly believe your home should be your sanctuary, where you surround yourself with every sensible and nonsensible thing you love, a place that speaks of where you've been and where you're going.

Make no mistake: Our homes are far from perfect! Just beyond the frame of every camera angle is a pile of dirty clothes, three half-unpacked suitcases, and a room still waiting to be decorated. Because that, my friends, is *real*. C'mon in anyway and stay awhile. Our hope is that you'll find an idea—a project, a picture, a spark of divine fire—that will inspire you. Because just like the wild woods or the glorious road, like fingerprints or feathers, *your* home is unique—and it should be uniquely *you*.

DIY ⊤⊤⊤⊤⊤⊤⊤ *Move Your Own House*

There once was an early 1900s farmhouse with no indoor plumbing, no electricity, and no people. We found this tiny cottage the way some people find a stray dog: lost on the side of the road, looking a little rough on the outside but with so much charm on the inside. It was small (about eight hundred square feet), but it had great bones. This house needed a home. It was begging for love, begging for a family of its own, and it had the potential to be the perfect home for Amie and Indie. So, like a humane society for stray houses, we picked it up and took it home with us.

1 Locate one history-rich house filled with a century or more of love, children, happiness, loss, laughter, music, and homemade bread.

2 Call burly types with big trucks.

3 Transport the house to your homestead and decorate to taste.

4 Insert family and live happily ever after.

AMIE'S HOUSE

I live in a little pink house. I always wanted to be able to say that.

My house is like a tiny little fairy tale, nothing very normal about it, but it's a place that feels like an escape. It's a lived-in house where there's glitter in every crack in the floor and crayons under the sofa. I think my theme, if I had to try and identify it, would be "wayward mermaid who joined the circus on her way through cowgirl country." (Yes, that's a real style, y'all. I learned about it in the design school I didn't go to.) It's vagabond world-weary traveler meets Annie Oakley. It's fun yet practical. In this tiny house, there's lots of room to dream. Indie and I couldn't be luckier. It's all about perspective. One day when she was four, Indie told me, "Mama, I love our house. We live in a mansion!" And I said, "Why yes!"

I think she is absolutely correct, and I love all eight hundred square feet of our "mansion."

Our trailers are always loaded with antiques and junk, but loading a trailer with an entire house—this was a first for us. Watching Kana Bros roust that thing up onto their big ol' truck was dinner and a movie—Texas-style. They inserted skids below the floor, hauled it onto the flatbed, and then—let 'er rip, tater chip!—this happy wanderer was on her way down the road.

Once she was settled on a solid foundation under a giant live oak tree in Gypsyville, her wandering days at an end, the little house got full-on Junk Gypsy salvation, inside and out. We added a porch made of salvaged table legs and gargantuan architectural corbels from the flea market and gave her a fresh coat of paint. Our little pink house (cue John Cougar Mellencamp) was a labor of love, and (like the rest of us) it's a work in progress.

Without a doubt, this was the biggest DIY we've ever tackled. I paid $17,000 for the house and about $4,000 to have it moved, so it's also the most expensive DIY we've ever done, but it's the cheapest house any of us have ever lived in. Indie and I found it while we were out for a Sunday drive, and within six months we were living in it. A few adjustments were needed. Like installing an indoor bathroom instead of an outhouse. Minor details like that.

THE LIVING ROOM COMBINES FARMHOUSE STYLE WITH WHIMSICAL FOUND TREASURES. WE VAULTED THE CEILING TO MAKE THE ROOM SEEM LARGER AND SET SHIP CHANDELIERS SAILING HIGH OVERHEAD. THE RED LEATHER CHAIR, ONE OF THE FIRST THINGS I EVER BOUGHT, CAME FROM A RANCH IN NEW MEXICO AND GOES PERFECTLY WITH A VINTAGE CAROUSEL PANEL. AN OLD ARCHITECTURAL HEADER BRINGS HEIGHT AND DRAMA TO A STANDARD DOOR FROM THE HARDWARE STORE.

THE MERMAID THEME CONTINUES
THROUGHOUT THE HOUSE WITH SEAFARING
MEMENTOS AND ART. ON THE WALLS ARE
MY MOST PRIZED FINDS FROM MANY YEARS
OF FLEA-MARKETING: CRUSTY OLD OCEAN
PAINTINGS, CRACKED MIRRORS, AND
DAVY JONES CERTIFICATES CELEBRATING
THE CEREMONY OF CROSSING THE LINE.
(FASCINATING! GOOGLE IT.)

JOLIE'S HOUSE

You know, I always wanted to live down a curvy, country gravel drive. One that has little sprouts of grass and wildflowers popping up in the middle. One that twists around a bend, with live oaks gently watching over like God's guardian angels, and wraps its way around my heart because it is . . . home. So this is our home, where all is right with the universe. Sometimes Todd and I sit on the front porch, looking out over the pasture, and I say, "I can't believe we made this happen." It's our personal Heaven, where our son, Cash Baker, can run free and climb trees and catch fireflies and go snipe hunting. It's where I can be everything I ever wanted to be: a farmer and a dreamer, eccentric and wild-hearted.

LEFT TO RIGHT ★ SIMPLE FARMHOUSE STYLE AND BASIC CONSTRUCTION ON THE CABINETS MEANT I COULD SPLURGE ON A WOLF STOVE. (YOU HAD ME AT RED KNOBS.) IT TAKES ME BACK TO HAPPY TIMES IN THE FAMILY RESTAURANT. ★ NONNEGOTIABLE WHEN TODD AND I BUILT THIS HOUSE: SLIDING BARN DOORS. DAD AND TODD MADE THESE TO SIZE, AND I STAINED THEM WITH MINWAX WOOD FINISH IN EBONY FOR VINTAGE EFFECT. THE GROCERY SIGN WAS A LUCKY FLEA MARKET FIND. ★ BIRDIE BLUEBELL, THE GOLDENDOODLE, AND JJ MCQUEEN, A SHELTER DOG, ADD TO OUR MENAGERIE OF GOATS, CHICKENS, CATS, AND THE OCCASIONAL CHURCH MOUSE.

ABOVE ★ THE RED VELVET TUFTED CHAIR IS A FAVORITE BOOK NOOK AND SANCTUARY
SPOT IN MY ECLECTIC KITCHEN. PAINTING THE HALLWAY WALL SHERWIN-WILLIAMS
REAL RED ADDED A BONUS POP OF COLOR. I COVERED THE KITCHEN CHAIRS WITH
RED BANDANAS. *LEFT* ★ I GOT FUN, KID-FRIENDLY TRACTOR SEATS ONLINE AND
1950s DINER STOOLS AS A HAND-ME-DOWN FROM MOM, WHO GOT THEM AT THE FLEA
MARKET, OF COURSE. *TOP LEFT* ★ THE ORNATE NINE-FOOT ISLAND CAME FROM THE
PEOPLE'S STORE IN LAMBERTVILLE, NEW JERSEY, WHICH I SCORED AT TEXAS ANTIQUES
WEEK.

DIY ⊤⊤⊤ *Jolie's Cabinets*

When I was building my house, I knew I wanted my kitchen to be very, very me. I wanted it to reflect my own unique style along with my love of old farmhouses. It would be the perfect paradox, a beautiful mishmash of old and new, unexpected choices with a traditional heart. I love my turquoise-stained cabinets. Stained, not painted, because I wanted to actually *see* the wood—every knot, all the whorled grains. It was a multistep process, and I lost a little sleep over the fact that I had never, ever seen turquoise cabinets before, but in the end—no guts, no glory!

1 If you're using old cabinets, remove the existing hardware and sand the cabinets completely to remove old paint.

2 Prepare the cabinets with a light coat of clear primer or conditioner.

3 Brush the cabinets on all sides with a coat of stain. I used Sherwin-Williams interior wood stain in Aquarius. For this project, it was important that the natural grain and whorls of the wood showed through, so I applied only one coat.

4 Allow the stain to dry completely, then apply a very thin coat of wood finish with a rag, rubbing it in completely as you go. (I used Minwax Provincial.)

5 Attach the hardware.

PITSTOP
Janie Sikes

Voice of Experience

Everything has a past. A history. Every piece of junk. This chandelier. That panel from an antique circus carousel. The enamel washtub that's bathed many a baby back in the black-and-white photo days. It's really all about perspective. To me, that history—the good, the bad, the ugly—makes each piece of junk better. It writes the story. To me, life is a lot like junk. Each of us has a history. For some, it's a tattered history. (I was a sorority girl dropout with a wild streak. Heck, I was a college dropout. But that's another story.) It's because of our history that we are who we are. We can choose to let that history make us better. We can pass on all the good stuff, like a good ol' piece of junk, to those willing to open their hearts and their homes to something with a story to tell. I never thought I'd be burning up the roads with my daughters buying and selling junk at this stage in my life, but I've started over again enough times in my life to know it doesn't kill you to fall down. And I guess my daughters missed the memo about how a grandmother is supposed to be growing tomatoes and sitting in a rocker on the front porch.

MOM'S HOUSE

They say home is where your mom is, and that will always be true in our hearts and souls.

THE HAND-PINNED SEQUIN DUCK DECOY IS ONE OF OUR FAVORITE FINDS. WE REPURPOSED A BIG BASS DRUM USING SALVAGED WOOD AS A TABLETOP. ★ THIS BEADED CHANDELIER IS NEW, BUT WE LOVE THE DRIPPY EFFECT IN THIS SPACE. ★ MOM IS THE QUEEN OF KNICKKNACK PADDY-WHACKS AND HAS HAD A LOVE OF VINTAGE JEWELRY AS LONG AS WE CAN REMEMBER.

PROJECT *Patchwork Fireplace*

Mom and Dad wanted an interesting fireplace as the focal point of their home, but it had to be something that also fit into their Texas-style farmhouse. We found an old corbel, split it down the center, and used it to flank either side. This stash of one-hundred-fifty-year-old Mediterranean tiles sang out to us when we saw it. If you're the patient type, keep your eyes peeled at flea markets, auctions, and yard sales. If you want instant gratification, you can always get mismatched salvage tile at tile shops and building surplus stores. Tile can be tricky, so seek out some solid advice from a friendly professional at your local hardware or home improvement store. Or take the path of least resistance and hire a mason. We topped the whole thing off with a beautifully irregular piece of cedar for a mantel. Behold, the patchwork fireplace. Christmas stockings never had it so good.

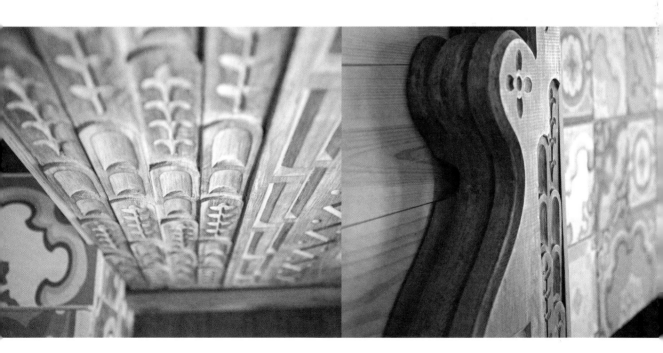

JG IS FAMILY

A few years ago, when Indie was only three, we were walking down the gravel driveway from our house to the store and she was adorably babbling about "*Jump Gypsy* this and *Jump Gypsy* that." It occurred to me that she might not really know exactly what Junk Gypsy is, though it is, in fact, the business that supports our very lives.

So I asked, "Baby, do you really know what Junk Gypsy is?"

To which she defiantly looked at me with her chubby toddler cheeks and said, "Mommy, I know what *Jump Gypsy* is since I was born!"

"Oh, really? What is it?"

And she said, "Mommy, *Jump Gypsy* is family!"

I couldn't have said it better.

Junk Gypsy *is* family in every sense of the word. Now that you're part of our family, we look forward to the moment when our wandering paths cross yours again.

Godspeed till then.

This book is more than just a book to us. It is a dream come true.

It is our story. Our life. Our family.

This process has not been easy. In fact, it's been anything BUT easy. We've stretched our brains in ways we didn't know possible; we've eaten frozen burritos every day for five months; we've agonized over every comma, every period, and every image to create something we are incredibly proud of. Something that we know reflects every aspect of Junk Gypsy to the core. We knew deep in our hearts that all of you die-hard Junk Gypsy supporters would settle for nothing less. We hope this book is something you can be just as proud of as we are . . . because we know Junk Gypsy is part of your very being. Just as it is part of ours.

With every ounce of our soul we would like to thank every single one of you who has been on this underground Junk Gypsy karma train with us for the past eighteen years. To the customers who have become friends, to our fellow vendors who have become partners in crime, to our JG crew who always have our backs. It's been a wild ride . . . and without y'all, Junk Gypsy might be stalled out on the side of the road somewhere. (Probably at a junk shop. And eating frozen burritos.)

To our parents, for all those backbreaking, exhausting days in the restaurant. For the sweat. The blood. The tears. For every arm burned on the pizza oven, for every dish washed, for every floor mopped, for every bathroom cleaned, for every holiday and weekend worked. We thank you. In some sick, twisted way, we thank you. This was our business school. Our MBAs. And we wouldn't trade it for anything. If our lives are a crazy quilt, you are the thread that holds it together.

To our kids, Indie and Cash Baker. Of all the adventures we've taken, nothing compares to being your moms. May your spirits always be wild.

To Todd. It takes a strong man to put up with us, and we're not just talking about your back and your biceps. You've always believed in our dreams, which you could not touch or feel, and for that we thank you. We'll be the first in line for your tell-all book.

To our JG crew—past and present—we LOVE you. Only you put up with our infinite Amazon packages and our tumbleweed brains. Only you understand the struggle to find Amie's desk on a daily basis and my innate need for avocados. Y'all are the awesomest group of badasses we know. **You are family.**

To the town of Overton and the town of Round Top. Thank you for being our Mayberry. Fayette County, thank you for welcoming us to your community even though we're not German or Czech and our last names don't have enough syllables . . . but we promise to eat sauerkraut and polka every chance we get.

To our flea market family, fellow vendors, and die-hard shoppers: You know who you are. Thanks for being on just this side of crazy with us from the beginning. Every last one of you. Only you can understand the adrenaline rush from a junk high, the glory of a cold beer after a long day setting up or breaking down, and the ethereal beauty of the flea market at night.

A very special group hug to the Zapp Hall gang: You took us in when JG didn't have a home and changed the course forever. Destiny is a beautiful thing. In the past fifteen years, our lives have changed immensely. We have cried together and laughed together. We are eternally connected by that little piece of land that means so much to all of us. You're stuck with us. Forever. (Sorry for that.)

To Ed Gage, Matt White, and Joe Pete for your personal accounts that helped tell our story.

Many photographers graciously contributed to this book and we really cannot thank you enough. Your images are magic and they truly capture the spirit of this story. To those who have been with us since the beginning: Courtney Christianson, Sam Franks, Keely Marie Scott, and Jack Thompson. Also, Matt Blair, Heather Bullard, Tomi Cheeks, Dixie Hamilton, David Stahl, and Sarah Wilson.

And of course, April Pizana, you have been broke down with us on the side of the road, you have weathered hurricane-force winds with us all for the sake of making a beautiful book and we thank you.

Joni and Jerusha: Oh, the magic you weave with bulk quantities of Post-it notes. Behold, the STICKY-GRID MOJO, without which we would have been lost. You were able to wrap your heads around a project that has seemed insurmountable to us for ten years. You tamed my ellipses and run-on sentences and Amie's infinite brainstorms. We could never thank you enough for your guidance, your organization, your help, and most of all, your patience and your friendship.

To the man brave enough to go down this road with us: Matthew Benjamin, you rock star, you. And to Simon & Schuster and Touchstone, thanks for taking a gamble on us Texas girls. Biscuits are forthcoming.

To Lorie and Kris for making this book as beautiful as we dreamed it could be. You crawled into Amie's head and into her doodle books and translated that magic into the pages of this book and for that, we are thankful.

To our book agent, John Howard, always our voice of reason. We thank you.

To HGTV, GAC, and Scripps Networks. To Dawn Fitzgerald and our entire film crew: We thought we had done it all until y'all came into our lives. Thanks for putting your lives on the line by inhaling glitter and sawdust on a daily basis.

To the Lambert family, the Robertson family, Marcus and Melanie Luttrell, Adrienne and Billie Joe Armstrong, and Dierks Bentley, thanks for letting us into your homes, your Airstreams, and your magnetic lives. We are infinitely inspired.

To our rogue board of directors: Rachel Ashwell, Mark Dooley, Mark Harkrider, Bev Lambert, David Morrison, Mark Sikes, and Jeremy Thompson. Who needs a boardroom when you have a dashboard?

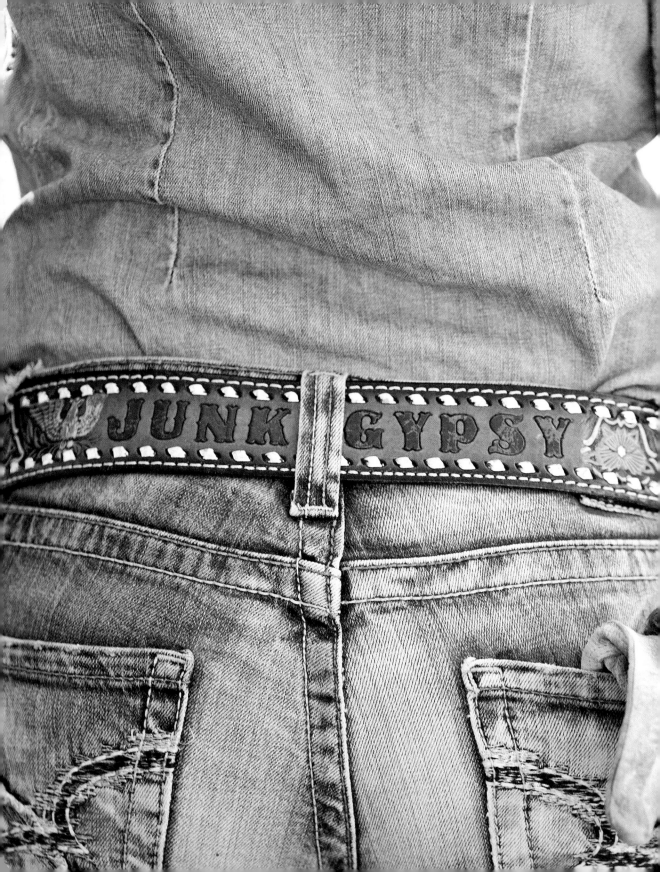

ABOUT THE AUTHORS

Born and raised in small-town Texas, **Jolie** and **Amie Sikes** graduated from Texas A&M University, but soon after realized the nine-to-five life was not for them. With only two thousand dollars and an old pickup truck, the Sikes sisters went on to launch the wildly successful Junk Gypsy brand and become the stars of two hit TV shows on HGTV and Great American Country. They have been featured in countless newspapers, magazines, and television shows, including the *Today* show, *Country Living*, *People Country*, *Southern Living*, the *Houston Chronicle*, *Fortune Small Business*, and more. In addition to curating and designing everything from clothing to housewares for their flagship store in Round Top, Texas (population: ninety), and online store, the sisters design a line for Pottery Barn Teen and have a line of Junk Gypsy paint and Lane Boots.

April Pizana graduated from the University of Houston–Clear Lake and taught middle school science for several years before she discovered her love for photography. Check out her current work on her blog at www .aprilpizana.com.

PHOTO CREDITS

April Pizana Photography: ii–iii; vi–vii; viii–ix; x; 2–3; 4; 8–9; 10–11; 18; 24–25; 26–27; 28 (top); 29 (right); 30–31; 36 (top right); 34–35; 40; 42; 43 (top row); 43 (bottom left and second from left); 45 (top row); 45 (bottom left and second from left); 46–47; 48–49; 51 (bottom); 52–53; 54 (bottom); 58–59 (middle); 60–61; 63; 67; 68–69; 70; 71 (right); 73 (bottom); 74–75; 79; 80; 83 (top right); 83 (middle right); 84–85; 90–91; 98; 100 (middle); 100 (bottom); 101 (top); 104 (bottom left and right); 105; 106 (bottom); 107; 108; 109; 110 (top right); 112; 113; 114 (right); 115; 116–117; 118–119; 124–125; 126; 128 (bottom); 129 (bottom left); 134 (top); 134 (bottom right); 135; 136; 137 (top right); 137 (bottom left); 138; 145 (top left); 145 (top right); 145 (bottom left); 146; 147 left; 147 (bottom right); 150–151; 152; 154–155; 156; 157 (middle); 157 (right); 163 (top right); 164 (top); 165 (top left); 170; 174; 175 (bottom left); 175 (top right); 175 (middle right); 177; 179 (bottom); 186; 188–189; 193 (top left and right); 190; 196–197; 203 (top); 206–207; 208; 210; 212–213; 215 (right); 216; 218; 219 (right); 220–221; 222; 223 (left and right); 225 (top left and second from left); 225 (third row left and third from left); 227; 228–229

Jolie Sikes: 6–7; 13 (top right); 20–21; 22; 23 (top row); 23 (middle row, second from left); 23 (bottom right); 29 (left); 38–39; 43 (bottom) 3–4; 44; 45 (bottom right); 58 (bottom right); 62; 64–65; 66; 71 (left); 71 (middle); 76; 81; 83 (top left); 83 (middle left); 83 (bottom); 86 (bottom); 87; 88 (left); 88 (middle); 94–95; 96–97; 101 (bottom); 102 (bottom); 103 (top right); 103 (bottom); 110 (middle right); 110 (bottom right); 111; 117 (bottom); 120; 122–123; 128 (top left); 128 (top right); 129 (top left); 139; 151 (bottom); 153; 157 (left); 158–159; 160; 165 (bottom left); 166; 167; 171; 175 (top left); 175 (bottom right); 176; 179 (top); 182–183; 184; 187 (top right); 187 (bottom right); 191; 192; 194–195; 198–201; 202; 203 (bottom); 204–205; 219 (left); 230

All other photographs courtesy of the Junk Gypsy family except: **Ken Amorosano:** 224; **Adrienne Armstrong:** 114 (top left); **Matt Blair:** 72; **Adrienne Buddin:** 54 (top right); **Heather Bullard:** 132–133; **Tomi Cheeks:** 50 (bottom); 140–141; 144; 145 (middle right); **Courtney Christianson:** 28 (bottom right); 57 (top right); 57 (middle right); 73 (top right); 103 (top left); 145 (middle left); 147 (top right); 149 (left); 225 (second row, second from the left); **Reed Davis Photography:** 172–173; 178; **Robert Evans:** 88 (right); **Sam Franks at Texas Star Digital:** 128 (middle); 137 (bottom right); 162 (bottom); 164 (bottom left); 165 (middle right); 165 (bottom right); **Kevin Grace:** 110 (top left); **Stefanie Graf:** 92–93; **Marion Kraft:** 169; **Dixie Hamilton at Dixieray Photography:** 129 (top right); **Bev Lambert:** 23 (middle left); 23 (bottom left); **Corey Rittenhouse:** 58 (top right); **Todd Sanders at Roadhouse Relics:** 50 (top); **Annie Schlechter:** 214; 215 (left); 217; **Keely Marie Scott:** 28 (bottom left); 51 (top right); 134 (bottom left); 137 (top left); 142; 145 (top right); 145 (bottom right); 148; 149 (right); 180–181; 225 (bottom right); **Stewart Smithson:** 102 (top); **David Stahl at antiqueweekend.com:** 36 (bottom); 58 (bottom left); 73 (middle right); **Jack Thompson:** 15; 32 (left); 32 (bottom); 33; 162 (top); 163 (bottom); 164 (bottom right)